A HISTORY OF
THE UNIFORMS OF THE BRITISH ARMY

General Officers.
1702-1714.

A HISTORY OF
THE UNIFORMS OF
THE BRITISH ARMY

BY

CECIL C. P. LAWSON

FROM THE BEGINNINGS TO 1760

VOLUME I

With many drawings by the Author

"EVERY TRIFLE EVERY
TAG OR RIBBON THAT TRADITION
MAY HAVE ASSOCIATED WITH THE
FORMER GLORIES OF A REGIMENT SHOULD
BE RETAINED, SO LONG AS ITS RETEN-
TION DOES NOT INTERFERE WITH
EFFICIENCY"
Col. Clifford Walton, C.B.

KAYE & WARD · LONDON

In association with Norman Military Publications Limited

First published by Peter Davis Limited
1940

Reprinted by
Norman Military Publications Limited
1962

Reprinted by Kaye & Ward Limited
194–200 Bishopsgate, London EC2
1969

SBN: 7182 0814 5

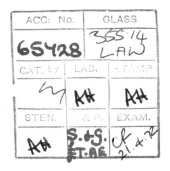
Printed in Great Britain by Butler & Tanner Ltd, Frome and London

FOREWORD

BY

THE MARQUESS OF CAMBRIDGE, G.C.V.O.

STUDENTS in all fields of British Army history will feel gratitude to Mr. Lawson for setting his hand to the vast task of giving us a complete and authoritative record of our Army's uniforms, of which this is the first volume. No previous author had ever attempted the task.

Other countries have long possessed such records. France has her Edouard Detaille, "Job" (the *nom de guerre* of J. O. de Bréville), Leinhardt and Humbert, Depréaux with his *Troupes de la Marine*, and many others; Germany has Mentzel, Knötel and others, with Anton Hoffman for the Bavarian Army of "Das Blauen Königs"; Austria has Rudolf von Ottenffeld and Oscar Teuber; Holland has van Pappendrecht. Russia, besides that of Pajol and others, has a voluminous and very complete work on all their uniforms; and there is *L'Armée Belge* by Colonel Rouen.

Nevertheless, long as we have had to wait for a comprehensive record of British uniforms to appear, a considerable mass of sound pioneer work (of which Mr. Lawson makes generous acknowledgement) has already been done. Colonel Clifford Walton's name must head this list of pioneers. His *History of the First Standing Army* covered only a part of our Army's history, and much fresh material has come to light since it was written, but it was a beginning. Questions of expense prevented the publication of his beautiful and painstaking illustrations; but his original water-colour drawings fortunately remain available to students in the Library of the Royal United Service Institution.

Other men to whom credit must be given for their spade-work are the Rev. Percy Sumner (whose researches have been so important that Mr. Lawson has rightly seen fit to include his name in the text), Major I. H. Mackay Scobie, Mr. Godfrey Brennan, the late Mr. P. W. Reynolds, Major Fitz-Maurice Stacke, and Mr. Hastings Irwin.

[v]

But it must not be thought that this work is no more than a co-ordination of the results of other men's researches. Mr. Lawson presents us with a large amount of hitherto undiscovered and unpublished material. A small but interesting detail of this sort is the evidence that the Royal Fusiliers, when first raised, wore aprons to protect their clothing from the ordnance it was their duty to handle. On the larger scale, soldiers from the mural paintings at Marlborough House are described and illustrated; as also the various vehicles of Marlborough's Train of Artillery, and many regimental colours of about 1700.

Subsequent volumes, of which I have been privileged to see the synopses, will give details of the uniforms worn by the Corps of Rangers and local Militia of the American Colonies previous to the Revolution, as well as the Militia units of other colonies. Thus the completed work will have an interest extending beyond the borders of the present British Empire.

Incidentally it is greatly to the credit of the author and his publishers not to be deterred by the present troubles from bringing out so ambitious a work, although its writing and preparation were begun long before we were once more forced to take up arms.

I should like to comment also on Mr. Lawson's particular fitness for writing this book. He is already well known as one of the few survivors of that once numerous band—painters of battle scenes. But his qualifications go much deeper than the mere ability to design a warlike scene with veri-similitude. For he has himself been a soldier, a cavalry soldier; and his personal knowledge of how a soldier feels under his red coat permeates his writing. At one point of this volume, he writes: "According to the military text-books of the time the orders to dismount and mount were executed by much the same drill movements as at the present time." Only a man who had learned mounting and dismounting by numbers in the riding-school could have written that sentence.

As I am myself keenly interested in the study of old military uniforms, I look forward to the day when the war is over and I shall be able to read all further volumes of this work from cover to cover.

CAMBRIDGE

B.E.F., France,
April, 1940

AUTHOR'S NOTE

IN the production of this book the question of cost has had to be continually considered; for this reason coloured illustrations have been kept down to a minimum; and colours (when known) described in the text, so that those who wish to colour the line drawings can do so.

The illustrations (except where noted) are all from contemporary sources, and closely copied from the originals whenever circumstances permitted.

To simplify the description of the development of uniforms of any period, the precedence of the various branches of the Army has not been followed, nor has it always seemed necessary to state that the unit was English, Scottish, Welsh or Irish, the term British being used in the widest sense.

As War was declared when the manuscript had not long been in the publisher's hands, and the final arrangement of the work, correction of proofs, etc., were done in hours off duty, it was not easy to check the various authorities and I therefore beg indulgence for any deficiencies.

ACKNOWLEDGEMENTS

I HAVE to express my dutiful gratitude to H.M. The King for the permission which was accorded to me to make use of the unrivalled stores of information contained in the Royal Library at Windsor Castle.

H.M. Queen Mary graciously allowed me access to the mural paintings at Marlborough House upon which so many of the illustrations in this volume are based.

I am greatly indebted to the Marquess of Cambridge not only for allowing me to consult his admirable collection of military books and prints, but also for the great amount of work which he contributed in particular to the portion dealing with the Hanoverian regiments.

Among those who have so kindly given their help I must thank especially the Rev. Percy Sumner who, besides other periods, has made a special study of the late 17th and early 18th centuries, and whose exhaustive researches have thrown so much light on this obscure period. His notes on the tapestries at Blenheim Palace have been particularly helpful.

Particular gratitude is also due to Major I. H. Mackay Scobie, Curator of the Scottish National Naval and Military Museum, for the advice and help he has so generously given in all sections dealing with Scottish troops and for allowing me to make use of the material contained in the invaluable collections in the Museum.

ACKNOWLEDGEMENTS

My grateful thanks are also especially due to: Her Grace the Duchess of Atholl, for permitting me to use the valuable information contained in her work *The Military History of Perthshire;* Messrs. Baldry and White and the Staff of the War Office Library; Mr. F. W. Barry, M.V.O., for his sketches and research made in the Royal Library, Windsor Castle; Mr. G. Brennan, for allowing me to consult his unique collection of military prints; Mr. Lionel E. Buckell, for supplying much valuable information from his collection of notes, photographs and sketches of uniforms; the Lieut.-Colonel Commanding the Grenadier Guards, for allowing me to consult the Order books of the regiment; Major C. J. ffoulkes, C.B., O.B.E., formerly keeper of the King's Armouries, and H.M. Office of Works, for generously supplying photographs of the models of the Train of Artillery, etc., and for granting permission to reproduce them; Colonel E. L. Hughes, D.S.O., O.B.E., and the Staff of the Royal United Service Institution; M. N. V. L. Rybot of the Museum of the Société Jersiaise, to whom I am indebted for the material dealing with the Jersey Militia; Herr Friedrich Schirmer, for allowing me to quote material from his works on the Hanoverian Army, *Nec Aspera Terrent* and *Das Celler Soldatenbuch*, besides supplying sketches of soldiers from contemporary drawings in Hanover; Mr. F. P. Todd and the American Military Institute, who have generously supplied all the notes and references to local American Corps collected from contemporary sources; and Mr. M. S. D. Westropp, M.R.I.A., for supplying much information concerning The Irish Corps.

For assistance of various kinds my grateful thanks are also due to: Mr. C. T. Atkinson, M.A.; Mr. E. W. M. Balfour-Melville, D.Litt., Scottish Historical Society; La Bibliothèque Nationale; the Bodleian Library; Lieut.-Colonel A. N. E. Browne; Mr. A. T. Butler, Windsor Herald; Captain E. A. Campbell; Mr. P. W. Clendenin; the College of Arms; Colonel C. de H. Crookshank, H.M. Body Guard, and King's Body Guard of Scotland; Brigadier-General E. A. Cruikshank, LL.D., F.S.C., F. R. Hist., Ottawa, Canada; Mr. William Cubbon, Director of the Manx Museum; Lieut.-Colonel W. W. S. Cunningham, D.S.O., H.M. Body Guard, and King's Body Guard of Scotland; Mr. Arthur Deane, F.R.S.E., M.R.I.A., Curator of the Municipal Museum, Belfast; Captain Druen; A. J. H. Edwards, Director of The National Museum of Antiquities of Scotland; Monsieur — Grangier; Colonel M. M. Haldane; the Viscount Harcourt; the Honourable Artillery Company; the Institution of Royal Engineers; Major-General Sir John Kennedy, K.B.E., C.B., C.M.G., D.S.O.; the King's Own Royal Regiment; Major A. J. R. Lamb, D.S.O.; Capitaine M. L. Leconte, Conservateur en Chef, Musée Royale de l'Armée, Bruxelles; Messrs. Leger & Son; Lieut.-General Sir G. F. MacMunn, K.C.B., K.C.S.I., D.S.O.; Major C. H. Massé, M.C.; Mr. O. F. Morshead, C.V.O., D.S.O., M.C., Librarian, Royal Library, Windsor Castle; Musée de l'Armée; Colonel F. S. Ormond, O.C., R.O.A.C. Records; General Dimitri d'Osnobichine; the Parker Gallery; Major H. G. Parkyn, O.B.E.; Mr. S. H. P. Pell, Director of The Fort Ticonderoga Museum; Mr. Olivier de Prat; The Prince Consort's Library; the Queen's Royal Regiment; Mr. E. J. Ruckerts; La Société de la Sabretache; Major H. S. Surtees; Major-General A. F. A. N. Thorne, C.M.G., D.S.O.; Major Tomlinson; The Rev. H. T. Tovey, M.A.; Major-General Sir I. L. B. Vesey, K.C.B., K.B.E., C.M.G., D.S.O.; Mr. A. J. B. Wace, M.A., F.S.A.; Major Gould Walker, D.S.O., M.C.; Major P. S. M. Wilkinson.

ACKNOWLEDGEMENTS

I am indebted to Captain Donald Anderson for much invaluable help, and for indexing this volume.

I am also greatly indebted to The Society of Army Historical Research, whose *Journal* is a veritable mine of information.

Mr. W. Y. Carman has done much careful and painstaking research work for me, besides supplying sketches of various items; his help has been invaluable in completing this volume.

Captain C. G. T. Dean has kindly allowed me to quote from his articles on the Royal Hospital, Chelsea.

Messrs. Macmillan & Co., Ltd., have kindly given their permission to quote from Sir John Fortescue's *History of the British Army*.

My friend the late P. W. Reynolds gave me his expert advice for many years and the use of material contained in his MS. volumes on the uniforms of the British Army.

Dr. Wilde has supplied me with much of the information relating to, and copies of pictures of, Dutch troops in the British Service and of the Scots Brigade in Holland.

With much of the information concerning *emigré*, Swiss and other similar Corps in the British Service, I have been greatly helped by my friend the Vicomte Grouvel, who has made the study of *l'emigration* his own and has generously allowed me to use any material contained in his voluminous notes. Messrs. Baldry and White have also been most helpful with this portion of the work.

To my many French friends I am indebted for permission to use English material in their collections and for the interest they have taken in my work.

Finally, I cannot express sufficiently my thanks to Messrs. Peter Davies Ltd. for their help and consideration in publishing this book under very adverse circumstances.

CECIL C. P. LAWSON

Royal United Service Institution,
      Whitehall
  May, 1940

B

CONTENTS

LIST OF ILLUSTRATIONS
With Notes on Sources, etc.

ILLUSTRATIONS

ILLUSTRATIONS

INTRODUCTORY

WHILE most nations have one or more works on the subject of the dress of their armies, our own army with its glorious history and ancient traditions has been strangely neglected.

In other countries there has always been a more or less continuous series of military artists who, in their efforts to obtain accuracy in their pictures, have collected uniforms, equipment, prints, etc., besides military studies and sketches of soldiers, so that not only was an interest in the subject maintained, but the public was familiarised to some extent with the dress of their armies at different periods.

The case in Great Britain, however, has been far different. For lack of any general history of the subjects, interest in the details of uniform has been almost exclusively regimental; moreover, we have had in the past very few painters of purely military subjects, and at the present time these have entirely disappeared. It is true that in 1916 it seemed as if we had to have a large and hitherto unsuspected supply, judging by the demands for the post of official war artist to the Forces, yet strangely enough since then none of them have continued to produce pictures of military subjects.

Now that full dress, with the exception of the Household Cavalry and the Foot Guards, seems finally to have disappeared and is now replaced by the mechanic's overall as the best effort in designing a soldier's dress, it seems that some record should be made of the dress of the Army which may serve to help artists, illustrators, costumiers and others interested in the subject. One was going to add film producers, but these, like the officer's batman, seem to have sources of information denied to other mortals. Much has been said of the cinema's educational possibilities and the opportunities offered by our history, but devoted bravery and stirring episodes carry no meaning to the great brains of this industry except in the form of the mawkish sentimentality of the novelette or the crudities of the knock-about comedian. Besides this, the ignorance on matters of dress and period is abysmal. Mounted orderlies of Wellington are shown in full infantry kit; the hussars of the Light Brigade in the Crimea carry standards; the lancers in the same Brigade wear a head-dress closely resembling the old-fashioned coal-scuttle; artillery of the Napoleonic period fire huge bombards similar to Mons Meg; the Highlanders at Fontenoy sport Glengarries and those at Waterloo are clothed in modern doublets. These are but a few of the gems presented with much pompous reference to careful research and enormous cost, especially the latter. It is true, however, that latterly the industry seems to have obtained the services of those with an expert knowledge of military matters, with satisfactory results. The stage, not to be outdone, has in recent years shown us Clive and his staff officers in the blue coat and distinctive shoulder-belt of the Garde du Corps of Louis XVI. The Press also adds

FIG. 1. Archer, 1346.

its quota to these inanities; only lately one leading Daily in reporting a State ceremony could give no better description of the Foot Guards than by drawing attention to "the tall fur busbies of the Life Guards."

Before studying uniform, in the present sense of the word as applied to troops of the regular army, it may be worth while to notice its early and rather vague beginnings.

Without going back to the subject of armorial bearings and badges, which were used to distinguish the knight and his retainers who followed him to the field, there are still many references which show that on some occasions at least an effort was made at a certain uniformity.

Edward III on one of his expeditions to the Continent ordered his archers to wear white jacks having the red cross of St. George on the breast and back (Fig. 1).[1] The French, it may be noticed, had the same device but with the colours reversed, the cross being white on a red field.

French authorities on archery, explaining the difference between the French and English longbow, point out that whereas the French archer with his weaker weapon was able to take steady aim and, like the sniper, pick off his

[1] Articles of War in *The British Fleet*, by Commander C. N. Robinson. Scottish troops had the white cross of St. Andrew before and behind.

enemy, the Englishman, whose more powerful bow could not be drawn for so long, depended upon shooting as many shafts as rapidly as possible at a certain distance and making it impossible for his opponents to advance, thus becoming the inventor of the *tir de barrage*. It is this that Froissart describes so aptly, when he says: "Then the English archers stepped forth one pace, and let fly their arrows so wholly together and so thick that it seemed to snow," and again at Poitiers "they shot so wholly together that none durst come within danger of them," as we may well believe when it is known that an expert archer could have six arrows in flight at the same time before the first had reached its target.

FIG. 2.
Man-at-Arms. 1458.

In 1470 a levy of men for the garrison of Calais were given red jackets decorated with white roses.

Warwick, on his attendance at the Great Council at Westminster in January 1458, was escorted by a body of 600 men of the garrison of Calais dressed in red jackets bearing the Beauchamp badge of the ragged staff (Fig. 2).[1]

With Henry VII we have the first body of permanent troops, which are with us to-day as the Yeomen of the Guard. They were then a body of picked men, chosen from the yeoman class, armed with bows and hand-guns, one half their number being mounted, the other serving on foot. They were given red livery coats. In the succeeding reign they are seen in contemporary pictures of the Field of the Cloth of Gold wearing red coats with full puffed sleeves with bands of black, the crown and Tudor rose being embroidered on the breast and back; puffed and slashed breeches and a flat cap completed their dress (Fig. 3). Beyond the coat, which has the same combination of colours but varies somewhat in the shape of the sleeve, there is a considerable variety in the colour and cut of the breeches and also in the colour of the caps and stockings. At the siege of Terouenne the archers of the corps wore white coats and caps.[2]

Some attempt was even made at this period to form a corps of drivers or waggoners for the Artillery teams. These were mustered and paid once a

[1] *Warwick the Kingmaker*, by C. W. Oman.
[2] Hall's *Chronicle*, sub anno 1513.

month and ordered to wear a white coat with the red cross.[1]

FIG. 3. Yeomen of the Guard. 1520.

Henry VIII in the thirty-sixth year of his reign ordered that:

"First every man souder to have a cote of blue cloth after such fashion as all footmens cotes be made here at London, to serve His Majesty's army on his journey, that the same be guarded with red cloth and the best sene to be trymed after such sort as shall please the captain to advise, provided always that no gentlemen nor other, wear any manner of silk upon the guard of his cote save only upon his left sleeve, and that no yeoman wear any manner of silk upon his sed cote nor noe gentleman nor yeoman to wear any manner of badge.

Every man to provide a pair of hoses, the right hose to be all red and the left hose to be bleu with one stripe of three fingers broad upon the outside of his leg from the hip downwards.

"Every man to have a cap to be made to put his salette in, after such fashion as I have desired, whibh William Taylor capper doth make for me, where you may have as many of them as you list for 8d. a piece."[2]

In most pictures and drawings of the period the cap is shown red.

Feudal badges were proscribed—"no soldier to bear no cognisance but the King's and his Captain's on pain of death. All to wear a St. George's cross." This was further emphasised by the fact that "anyone murdering a soldier not wearing the cross of St. George" or, in other words, in non-royal uniform, was not to be punished.

A series of contemporary coloured drawings of the army of Henry VIII show that the cross of St. George was no longer, as a general rule, placed large upon the breast and back, but worked as a border or

---

[1] Fortescue's *History* (*see* Bibliography).   [2] MS. College of Arms, marked W.S. (folio 240). S. S.

band to the lamboys or scattered over the coat or cloak (Figs. 4, 5, 6).[1]

In one of the drawings showing Henry's army in battle array a strong force of armoured cars or war carts are to be seen. These are rectangular structures of thick wood like a small fort, the sides of which come down so as to cover the wheels as well as the horses, which are inside, and of course supply its mobility; to make the comparison with present-day tanks more complete, these war carts carried small pieces of cannon.

The dress of Henry's army at Boulogne is thus

FIG. 4.   FIG. 5.

Soldiers, Henry VIII.

described:

"In the Vanguard passed 12,000 footmen and 500 light horse clothed in blew Jackets with red guards (facings, or rather trimmings).

"The middle ward (wherein the King was) consisted of 12,000 footmen and 2,000 Horsemen clothed in red jackets with yellow guards.

"In the rear ward was the Duke of Norfolk, and with him an army of like number and apparel, saving therein served one thousand Irish all naked save their mantles and their thick gathered skirts. The arms of the latter were three darts or javelins, a sword and a skene."[2]

In Queen Mary's reign we find a mention of a levy of troops dressed in white jacks decorated with the cross of St. George.

FIG. 6. Soldier, Henry VIII.

[1] Cotton MS., Aug. III.   [2] *Relation of the Most Famous Kingdomes*, 1630.

A HISTORY OF THE UNIFORMS OF THE BRITISH ARMY

A letter of 1557 concerning the clothing of a body of men for service in the Highlands says "their coats must be after the old manner, that is white coats and red crosses, for so my Lords think most fit." (*Ref. History of the Ordnance.*)[1]

In Elizabeth's time we come across a number of descriptions of the dress given to bodies of troops. These vary according to the arm to which the men belonged. Thus, in the quotas of certain Hundreds to supply men in 1559, we find a levy of 200 soldiers and 267 pioneers. The dress of the latter is to be "a cassock of watchett (pale blue) a yard ¾, a white doublet, white hose, shoes, garters and points, a scull and cap, a sword, dagger and girdle."[2]

In 1566 the archers sent from Liverpool to Ireland wore blue cassocks with two small guards of white cloth. The Staffordshire contingent wore red and the other detachments blue. The following year the men sent from Yorkshire were in light blue with two small laces, red caps and buckskin jerkins.[3]

A muster proclamation, Liverpool 1567, states that "Every man is to have a cassock of blue watchett Yorkshire cloth guarded with two small guards stitched with two stitches of blue apiece, a very good yew bow and a shief of arrows in a case a red cap, a stag or buckskin jerkin, a sword dagger and every man to have 13s. 4d. in his purse." (*Ref. Liverpool Town Records.*)

An entry of 1573 describes a brawl between the "blue coats" of Captain Roger Sydnam and the "motley coats of another captain."

In 1569 a corps of arquebusiers raised at Salisbury wore blue coats and red caps. In 1574 the coats of the infantry were to be blue, cut in the Gascony fashion, at a cost of 12/4, hose, shoes, shirt and doublet. Artificers coats to be red Gasconie fashion, tied under the arms with white ickle (tape).[4]

A body of Artificers raised in Lancashire in 1576 for service in Ireland were to be clothed in cloth coats made in the fashion of a cassock and guarded with two laces of crulls (crewel or worsted lace), the one red and the other green colour.[5]

A levy from Lancaster in 1577 wore the following dress:

"The Pikemen a coat of blue Yorkshire broad cloth with two stripes of red and yellow broad cloth by way of border; a vest of Holmes fustian, pale blue kersey shirts with two stripes of red or yellow cloth down the seams two

[1] Talbot Letters, College of Arms, Vol. D.   [3] Harl MS. 1926, Ar. ix and Ar. x.   [4] Ibid.
[2] Sir Sibbald Scott's *British Army*.   [5] Harl MS. 1926, Ar. ii, folio 90.

fingers broad with garters and points, stockings of white kersey, shoes with large ties, the coat to be cut Gascony fashion, the breeches Venetian (i.e., full breeches coming over the knees)."[1]

The archer was dressed in the same way, with a scull and a Scottish cap to cover it. The Pioneers to have cassocks or coats of the same colour, but not of broad cloth, their vests and breeches to be white. They were to have sculls and caps like the archers and to be armed with a sword and dagger.[2]

The colour of the Canterbury troops was yellow, which was changed to red in 1590.

The Norwich troops in 1587 wore coats of bayes and cursey laced with white tape. The drummers' coats were green cursey (or kersey) and ornamented with 11 yards of lace and six of pointing.[3]

1580. The cavalry to be furnished with "red cloaks lined and without sleeves of a length to the knee, doublets, hose, hatts, boots and all other necessary apparel."[4]

Colonel Field in his interesting book, *Old Times under Arms*, quotes the two following descriptions, the first from Old Sandwich Records and the other from contemporary letters.

When Queen Elizabeth visited Sandwich, a body of three hundred troops was drawn up to receive her dressed "in whyte doblets with black and whyte rybons on the sleeves, black gascoyne hose and white garters, eury of them having a muryon and a calyver; haveing thre dromes and three ensignes."

The Yorkshire levies of 1587 to have "their cassocks and breeches of blue cloth guarded with yellow."

1585. A body of troops raised at the expense of the City of London were given red coats for service in the Low Countries.

The red cassock seems to have been generally worn by the troops under John Morris, Sir Philip Sidney, Lord Willoughby, Sir Francis Vere and others, who played a large part in freeing the Low Countries from the Spanish yoke. On one occasion a Spaniard is described as having approached unchallenged close to the English lines by wearing a red cassock stripped from a dead soldier. One famous regiment, the Buffs, traces its origin to these corps in Dutch service, and was, in fact, long called the Holland Regiment (Fig. 7).

---

[1] Harl MS. Lancashire Lieutenancy, p. 89.
[2] Ibid.
[3] Norfolk Archeology i, pp. 6 etc.
[4] Desid. Curioso I, iii, 22.

Apparently for service in Ireland these red and blue coats were not found suitable, as what might be called a service kit was ordered to be worn, the colours to be "sadd green or russet" with a short cloak for protection against the weather.

FIG. 7. Musketeer, *c.* 1588.

A bill for clothing[1] dated 7th Feb. 1625 gives some details of the dress of the Guards of James I:

Red cloth for rich coats of the Guards	£450
For embroidery of sadd coats	667
Fine gold and silver for spangles for same	2,926
To tailor for making the same	220
	£4,263

In General Forbes' *History of the Ordnance Services* are the following lists, which are of interest for the details they give:

"1642. Monmouth caps, doublets, coats or cassocks of Suffolk, Coventry or Gloucester cloth and breeches of Reading or other cloth both shrunk in cold water, stockings of good welsh cotton, shoes, shirts, etc."

The Monmouth cap is also mentioned in the slop clothing lists for seamen. From the pictures and also an actual cap in existence it seems to have been on the lines of the brewer's or fisherman's cap. The actual specimen has a rough

[1] Yeomen of the Guard.

appearance and the "bag" is fairly long, in fact the forerunner of the grenadier cap. One agreement states that the coats are to be made "3 quaters and a nail long (27¼ inches) faced with bayes or cotton with tape strings according to a pattern delivered to the committee and breeches in length three quarters ⅛th (31½ inches) well lined and trimmed suitably to the pattern presented." General Forbes remarks that "these lengths are those of a modern full-dress tunic and knickerbockers for a man of average height."

Charles I standardized equipment, and arms and firelocks were to be repaired by expert armourers, as it had been found that many of the muskets had been damaged by tinkers and other unskilled persons. No armour or arms were sold without being marked with the stamp of the Company of Armourers.

During the Civil War the troops on both sides must have begun to have more or less the appearance of being uniformed. This, no doubt, was partly owing to Colonels taking the opportunity of buying up large quantities of cloth at a cheap rate when the occasion presented itself and so enabled them to provide better material for clothing their men at less expense to themselves. This, in general, seems to have applied only to the coats; in other respects the men, no doubt, dressed as best they could. It is true, however, that red breeches seem to have become the sign of a soldier, from one or two references to them in contemporary writings about this time.

A letter of 1638 may be quoted in support of this. "It would be good if Yr. Lordship's men had red breeches to their buff coats, because otherwise being country fellows they will not be so neatly habited as the other Lord's men."

In a list of the general muster behind Wadham College in February 1645 the following regiments and their coats are given:

The King's Life Guards, red coats
The Queen's Life Guards, red coats
Lord Percey's, white coats
Col. Charles Gerard's regt., blue coats
Col. Pinchbeck's regts., grey coats

Another list of the Royal Forces, in the year 1644, gives:

1st Regt., King's Life Guards, Col. Earl of Lindsay (no coats mentioned).
2nd Regt., Lord Hopton's, blue coats

FIG. 8. Pikeman, 1642. "Charge your Pike."

3rd Regt., Col. Aspley's, red coats
4th Regt., Col. Talbot, yellow coats
5th Regt., Col. Ashley's (no coats mentioned)
6th Regt., Col. Cooke (no coats mentioned).[1]

We have here drawn some of these regiments' colours, as they are examples of the conventions then in use and of which we will speak further on.

The above regiments are infantry. There is no mention of the dress of the cavalry, but these were generally dressed in buff coats, breastplates and the lobster tail helmet. Superior officers only would wear the demi-armour, which was by this time falling into disuse, although from a contemporary description, one of the Parliamentary regiments seems to have been so heavily armed "in their bright iron shells" as to have been called Hazelrig's Lobsters by the Royalists.

Prince Rupert also had a regiment of Foot Guards clothed in scarlet.[2]

The following regiments are mentioned in the Civil War:

"Denzill Lord Robert's, red coats

"Lord Saye's, blue coats

"Colonel Ballard's, grey coats

"Lord Brooke's, purple coats

"Colonel Hampden's, green coats

"Sir William Constable's, blue coats

"Colonel Meyrick's, grey coats

"Newcastle's, white coats

"Sir John Suckling's Troop wore white doublets, scarlet coats and hats with scarlet feathers."[3]

With both sides wearing the same coloured coats it was necessary to have some distinguishing badge, and scarves were often used for this purpose. At

[1] Symonds' Diary, B.M. MSS. Room.
[2] Symonds' Diary, 19a. B.M. E. 303.
[3] Sibbald Scott, *British Army*, Vol. I, p. 460; Vol. II, pp. 446-447.

INTRODUCTORY

Edgehill, for instance, the Royalists wore white while Essex's army had orange.

At the siege of Bristol Prince Rupert ordered his men to wear green colours, either bows or such like, and every officer and soldier to be without any band or handkerchief about his neck.[1]

The "New Model" adopted a red coat for the uniform of its regiments. The regiments "were only distinguished by their facings; Lt.-General Fairfax's having blue," states a newspaper dated April 30, 1645.[2]

An exception was made in the case of two companies of Firelocks, who acted as escort to the Train of Artillery, who wore coats of tawny. It is interesting to note that these companies of Firelocks were carrying out the same duties for which the Royal Fusiliers were raised later.[3]

The gun carriages of this Train were painted a "fair ledd colour."*[4]

For the army sent to Ireland by Cromwell orders were given for "15,000 cassocks of Venice-red colour shrunk in water," the like number of pairs of breeches of grey or other good colour, 10,000 hats and bands, 1,000 iron griddles, 1,500 kettles.[5]

According to Planché Cromwell had a personal guard of Halberdiers dressed in grey coats guarded with black velvet.

The British contingent under Morgan serving with the French army commanded by Turenne "were conspicuous in their red coats."

At the funeral of Oliver Cromwell in November, 1658, his son gave the foot soldiers about London new red coats guarded with black for the occasion. This custom of giving black facings as a sign of mourning we shall see repeated at a later date.

The foregoing notices of dress are sufficient to show that an attempt at uniformity in dress had begun, although it is not to be taken for granted that this was the case throughout the military forces in general, knowing as we do the hasty and haphazard way Commanders raised their corps.

[1] *Rupert Prince Palatine*. Eva Scott. [2] Sir John Fortescue's British Army newspaper, 1645. [3], [4], [5] Ibid.
* "Ledd colour," actually red lead, which was more or less the universal colour gun carriages were painted.

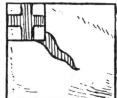

FIG. 9. Colours of the City of Oxford Regiment, 1644.

[11]

VALENTINE'S DAY, 1660.

INFANTRY

ALTHOUGH the thorough regularisation of military uniform may be said to date from the reign of Charles II, in studying the periods of 1660–1714–1735 we are still on somewhat uncertain ground as regards regimental dress. True, there are a certain number of engravings and paintings of the period, but these give only a rough and general idea of the soldiers' dress and very little which one can take as being that of any identifiable regiment.

In the advertisements for deserters, clothing bills, personal letters and other documents of the period, a certain amount of regimental detail is to be found, but even this leaves the arrangement of lace, facings, design of the horse furniture, etc., almost entirely a matter of conjecture. Portraits again, with one or two exceptions, are of very little use owing to the convention of the sitters being portrayed in armour. For the Marlborough campaigns we have very little pictorial evidence with the exception of the paintings by Laguerre at Marlborough House and the tapestries at Blenheim Palace. These, as was customary in paintings of that time, show mostly generals and staff officers, the actual regiments generally appearing rather vaguely in the background. These paintings and tapestries were made by order of the Duke and are therefore very nearly contemporary, although they must have been completed some time after the events depicted. The paintings at Marlborough House give the impression of showing a somewhat later style of dress than the Blenheim tapestries, possibly more that of 1720 than 1704–12. In making my drawings for this period I have for this reason compared them with the prints, etc., of other countries and based my reconstruction on a slightly earlier type of dress.

Dr. Stuart Reid in his *John and Sarah* gives the following information and dates of these tapestries. Almost as soon as Blenheim began to be built in 1705 the Duke decided that de Vost should depict his battles and appears to have given the commission in 1706. In 1713, the Duchess being abroad, the Duke wrote asking her on passing through Brussels to visit Monsieur de Vost and see the tapestries. From this we can see that these tapestries, begun in 1706, are consequently contemporary evidence.

With the return of Charles II from Holland commences the actual origin of the regiments of the regular army, Monk's regiment, which had marched from Coldstream on the Tweed, being first taken into the service of the King on his return to England.

The account of the disbanding of the Lord General's regiment of Foot and Life Guard of Horse, the last of the Parliamentary army, and their re-enlistment in the service of the Sovereign is thus described in the *Mercurius Publicus*:

"Westminster, Feb. 20th 1660. On Thursday the 14th February the Commissioners disbanded the Lord-General's Regiment of Foot and Life Guard of Horse on Tower Hill (being the only remaining land forces of the army) with more than ordinary solemnity. Sir William Doyley, William Prynne esquire, Col. Edward King and Colonel John Birch, four of the Commissioners sent from Westminster in a coach to Tower Hill about ten o'clock on Thursday the 14th of this instant (being Valentine's Day) where the Lord-General's Regiment of Foot and Life Guard appearing with their arms before them, they ordered five companies of the Foot to draw up in a ring about Mr. Prynne, and the other five about Col. Birch, who made two short speeches to them to this effect—'That God had highly honoured them in the eyes and hearts of the King and Kingdom, yea, and made them renowned throughout the world and to all posterity in stirring them up to be eminently instrumental in the happy restoration of His Majesty to his Royal Throne, the Parliament to their privileges and our whole three Kingdoms to their ancient laws, liberties and government without battle or bloodshed, for which signal services His Majesty and the whole Kingdom returned not only their verbal but real thanks the King having freely given them one weeks pay by way of gratuity over and above their wages and the Parliament and Kingdom provided monies for their just arrears, which upon disbanding should be forthwith paid for their use into their officers hands. That this regiment as it was the first of all the army who promoted his Majesty's glorious restoration to his Crown so it hath this signal badge of honour now put upon them to be the last regiment disbanded; and although they were ordered and declared to be disbanded in relation to the Kingdom's pay, yet they were immediately to be advanced to His Majesty's service as an extra-ordinary Guard to his Royal person, whom God long preserve in health and happiness,' which speaches being ended, they all cried out with reiterated shouts and acclamations 'God save King Charles the Second,' waving and throwing up their hats, displaying their ensigns, beating their drums and discharging their muskets over and over until commanded to draw off to their respective colours, when they were called over and disbanded by Mr. Prynne, Col. King and Col. Birch, Mr. Prynne causing all those five companies he disbanded to lay down their arms at his feet in testimony of their disbanding and then to take them up again as entertained by his Majesty in service.

"The same ceremony took place with the Life Guard of Horse, most of whom are since entertained by His Majesty for his Horse Guards."[1]

Infantry regiments before the Restoration were composed of equal numbers of musketeers and pikemen, but on the return of Charles II the number of pikes dropped to one third. This proportion of pikemen gradually grew less with the improvement of the musket and the introduction of the bayonet, until at last it was only fourteen men per company.

[1] Later the Royal Horse Guards.

INFANTRY

At first the dress of the musketeers was a short jacket, which a few years later became longer until by the end of the century it reached nearly to the knees.

FIG. 10. Pikeman's Pot.

In its early form it may have had a very small cuff, which gradually developed into a much wider and fuller shape, although during the period under consideration it does not appear to have attained the proportion in the British army that it did abroad.

In the early part of Charles's reign the musketeer seems at times to have worn a buff coat over his uniform jacket. A picture at Hampton Court, representing the departure of Charles II from Holland, shows a regiment which is very probably Wentworth's regiment of Foot Guards (afterwards the Grenadier Guards). They are dressed entirely in scarlet with a buff coat, the sleeves of which are thrown back and left hanging loose, showing the red of the underjacket. All wear helmets or pots except the officers and drummers who have hats. An officer who appears to belong to the regiment is dressed in a blue coat with gold lace edging down the front and on the pockets and loops of the same round the bottom of the skirts, red breeches and stockings, and a laced hat with red and white plumes (Fig. 11).

FIG. 11. Foot Guards, 1660.

On the title page of Captain Venn's book, *Military Observations*, published in 1672, a musketeer is shown dressed in a similar way.

Hollar in his sketches shows the coat as a frock-like garment, hanging loosely and without being shaped to the waist, with a single row of buttons down the front. Later on it seems to have a more shaped appearance, but this may be due to the introduction of the waist belt about 1680.

By the end of the seventeenth and beginning of the eighteenth century it had become distinctly shaped to the body, having full skirts with pleats at the sides. A feature of the period is the large quantity of buttons used. At times the top of the coat is shown unbuttoned and turned back, giving the effect of a small lapel.

Although many of the regiments wore red coats this was by no means universal, as many corps wore grey and others blue. The Lord High Admiral's Maritime Regiment, a forerunner of the Royal Marines, wore yellow coats faced with red and red breeches and stockings. The frequent use of grey cloth was no doubt due to the facility of procuring home-spun.

One must remember that at this time there was nothing in the nature of Dress Regulations or Government Clothing Stores. Colonels were responsible for the clothing of their men and took a good deal of license in their view of the matter. They made agreements personally with the tailors for the supply of all garments, hence the considerable variations of uniform between different regiments. In some cases it seems that the colours of the uniform adopted were based on those of the Colonel's coat of arms.

Colonel Clifford Walton quotes a curious case of Lord Chesterfield on raising his regiment in 1667 giving his soldiers red coats lined black and flags with a red cross on a black field "which I then did because I was at that time in mourning for my mother."

While on this subject the following order, issued by the Duke of Marlborough in 1708, also appears to refer to mourning dress:

"Colonels of Regiments in Flanders by desire of His Grace the Duke of Marlborough are to give directions to all officers of their respective regiments to have red coats with black buttons and button holes for their respective regiments clothing for the present year.

"Whitehall, 16 March 1708–9."

INFANTRY

At the beginning of Charles II's reign the fall down linen collar was still in use, but was soon to be replaced by a white neck-cloth which was knotted and the ends either left hanging down or tucked into the top of the coat.

From about 1686 to 1689 what seems to have been a sort of undress coat of grey, faced generally grey or black, is mentioned. There were no overcoats, only a few watch coats were issued for night guards. Surtouts have often been taken to mean overcoats, whereas they appear at times to have been some form of undress kit and at others the actual uniform coat.

As a matter of fact a good deal of uncertainty obscures the true meaning of the references to these grey coats and surtouts. In the French and other Continental armies the surtout was the outer uniform coat worn over the "veste," which was what might be described as a sleeved waistcoat into which garment it finally developed. This may account for the various discrepancies in the description of regimental dress. As an example may be cited the Inniskilling regiment of Foot where in one place we are told it was grey and in another list of clothing of the same date it is given as red. It seems fairly certain, however, that in some regiments there existed a sort of undress or fatigue coat.

A good instance of this is Farrington's Regiment, later the 29th Foot, which was raised in 1694. On 30th January of that year a contract was made between Colonel Thomas Farrington and Thomas Plummer, weaver, and James Gutheridge, tailor, for the supply of "754 surtout coats of white kersey faced with yellow for the Private Sentinels and Corporals and as many pairs of breeches of blue kersey to tye below the knee as likewise 39 surtout coats and breeches for the Sergeants and 26 Surtout coats of yellow kersey faced with blue bays and as many pairs of breeches for the Drummers." On the 26th March of the same year another contract was signed between Colonel Farrington and James and Stephen Pigou, merchants, to supply clothing and equipment. This list includes, besides coats and breeches, shoes, stockings, hats, shirts, neck cloths, swords and belts and snapsacks. The Grenadiers' lists having a cap and a match box over and above the articles for the musketeer. The Pikeman had a shoulder belt for his sword and was furnished with a hat.

On comparing the prices of the two contracts one finds that in the first list the men's white surtout coats cost 14/- each, whereas in the Pigou's estimate the price was £1 18s. od.

In the *Gazette* of 1696 is an advertisement for two men of the same regiment who deserted in their regimentals, viz: red coats with brass buttons lined and faced with yellow, blue breeches and white stockings. It seems possible, therefore, that the white and yellow surtouts were for drill, fatigues, etc., while the more expensive article, the red coat, was for full dress occasions.

Hollar, who went to Tangier and made a series of drawings of the town, its fortifications and harbour, has left us an invaluable and vivid record of an

FIG. 12. Officers, Sergeant and Privates, Tangier.

overseas garrison of 1669. On studying these watercolours the impression that will surely come to those of us who have had experience of similar outlying stations is that the passing of over two hundred and fifty years has wrought little change. All is there—the reliefs and ration parties are seen going to the outposts, fatigue parties at work on the defences, cavalry patrols are on the move. For the men off duty a bowling alley takes the place of the present-day football ground as a means of relaxation.

That the similarity may be complete, there was the usual clamour of ecclesiastics and short-sighted politicians which caused this early colonial possession to be ignominiously abandoned.

But let us turn to the men who formed the garrison and who, to quote the words of Lord Dartmouth "truly were soldiers who sought their bread where finer gentlemen would not vouchsafe to come." The officers are shown wearing what may be called a service dress consisting of a coat, waistcoat, breeches, stockings, shoes and hat, all of grey. The hat is somewhat lower in the crown and smaller in the brim than was usual. The sash is replaced by a cord round the waist, which is the same colour as the knots of ribbons on the shoulders, shoes and knees, in the hat and on the neckcloth. The baldrick seems to be of some material of the same colour as the ribbons (Fig. 12). The whole dress was, no doubt, an attempt to design a lighter clothing for

Fig. 13. Soldiers, Tangier.

the hot climate. Figures which appear to be sergeants by their carrying halberds are also in this grey uniform, but with red cuffs, while the men are wearing their red coats with cuffs of facing colour. Many of the privates have red coats and blue facings, stockings and breeches, and others with the same articles of dress a green colour. The breeches are often of a brownish tone, possibly to represent canvas. The hats are often brown, high in the crown and wide-brimmed (Fig. 13).

We get still further information about this garrison of Tangier from a set of oil paintings now in the National Maritime Museum, Greenwich. One is especially interesting as it shows the whole force drawn up for a review or parade held in honour of the Alcalde Omar. To increase the display of force the seamen from the king's ships were dressed in the soldiers' uniforms and took part in the parade. All the regiments are clothed in red coats (except one in grey) and the stockings in many cases seem to be red; cross belts of buff are the equipment for every unit. The pikemen are also in red and appear to be without any defensive armour. The drummers in every case wear the same dress as the rest of the battalion. The figures are very small and details like facings, etc., are not distinguishable. The composite battalion of Guards and the Royal Scots are both in red and are identifiable by their colours. Four small figures of pipers are to be seen in one painting, and are dressed like the battalion and not in Highland costume. The officers of the different regiments are not very uniform in their dress, as some are dressed in red and others in grey or buff coats.

One detachment appears to be a company of grenadiers judging by their low fur caps with red bags or hoods. In another of these pictures two officers and a soldier are painted on a considerably larger scale and show more detail. One officer has a whitish felt hat with a white ribbon and bow, fringed white waist sash, blue cuffs edged silver and blue breeches. The other officer is much the same only he wears a black silver-edged hat, blue stockings, buff waist belt and carries a half pike. The private seems to be of the same regiment as his uniform is similar.

These paintings were done at a later date than Hollar's, and the difference in the style of dress is distinctly noticeable.

At the Restoration the hat was buff coloured and high crowned like that worn during the Commonwealth. This was changed for one of black felt with a lower crown, round the base of which was tied a band of ribbon and knot of the facing colour. The brim, which was narrower than formerly, was often bound with white or yellow tape, or at times, as in the case of the Foot Guards and Horse, with gold or silver galloon. It became customary to loop one or both sides until about 1698 to 1700, when the three sides were turned up, forming the three-cornered hat, but not the regular symmetrical shape of later date. The point is sometimes shown worn at the back (Fig. 14).

FIG. 14. Hats, c. 1660–1712.

The breeches of infantry were at first very full, and ornamented occasionally with a row of buttons down the sides. They were tied below the knee with ribbons; stockings and shoes tied with ribbons or, in the case of officers,

FIG. 15. Hats and Wigs, c. 1705.

with a rosette, completed the leg coverings. The breeches seem to have become less baggy, and the stockings were pulled over the knees and kept up by a strap and buckle. The shoes towards the end of the century were fastened also with a strap and buckle.

On the Continent a thicker and coarser pair of stockings was worn on service or in marching order to protect the finer ones, the former being drawn over the knees and the latter pulled up under the breeches at the knees. Owing no doubt to the unsuitability of shoes and stockings for campaigning in the mud of the Low Countries, gaiters, or spatterdashes as they were called, came into use during the Wars of the Spanish Succession. In 1691 100 pairs of gaiters were ordered for Belcastle's regiment of Foot, but it is a question in this case whether these spatterdashes were really gaiters or the heavy over-stockings just mentioned.

The men's hair is shown in pictures and engravings of the period as being worn long or rather what in modern parlance would be termed "a long bob." This is sometimes shown tied in the middle at the back of the neck with a piece of string or ribbon to keep it from blowing about.

James Douglas when Colonel of the Scots Regiment of Foot Guards in 1684 made all his men "ty the hair back with a ribbon" so that it did not blow into their eyes when firing.[1]

Although the hair bag is not shown in any pictures until towards the end of the reign of Queen Anne, and then generally for the cavalry, we shall find that it was already used by infantry in the reign of William III.

The officers wore the full flowing curled wigs then the mode, but on service we see that these were plaited up in various ways, as, for example, in two pigtails knotted (Fig. 15).

Both officers and men were clean-shaven, although a few officers, especially in the early part of the reign of Charles II, are shown wearing small

[1] Fountainhall's *Historical Notices*.

FIG. 16. Officers, 1688.

moustaches. It is also possible that some, while on active service, may have left the upper lip unshaven, as is noticeable in the portrait of Lord Stanhope, where he is painted in uniform, whereas in his other portraits in civilian dress he is clean-shaven.

The dress of infantry officers was somewhat similar to that of the men, but of better material, and was laced down the seams at the back and on the sleeves with gold or silver. The buttonholes had gold or silver embroidery or loops (Fig. 16).

At first a knot of ribbon was worn on the right shoulder, which, it has been suggested, was an early form of epaulette. It may be noted that it is very rare to see in contemporary paintings officers' coats with cuffs of the regiment's facing colour; they are nearly always the same colour as the coat.

In the French Army at this time and for long after there was considerable difficulty in getting officers to wear the uniform of their regiments and, if worn at all, it would only have been by the junior officers.

Sashes were worn at first over the shoulder, but this position was soon changed to round the waist (Fig. 16). They were generally, but not invariably, of crimson and often interwoven with gold or silver with fringes of the same. The sword was carried in a baldrick, which was richly embroidered and fringed with gold or silver, but this, too, gave place to a waist belt (Fig. 16). Besides their swords officers carried half pikes or spontoons, and on the occasion of a ceremonial parade the Colonel himself would dismount and, carrying a half pike (Fig. 16), lead his regiment on foot past the Sovereign or Prince who was present.

The gorget which, with the exception of the cuirass, was the last piece of mediæval armour to be worn, was of considerable proportions and seems to have protected the shoulders to a certain extent. It soon diminished in size,

| FIG. 17A | FIG. 17B | FIG. 17C |
| Pikeman's Gorget, James I | Officer's Gorget, William III, and Queen Anne. | |

however, and was worn tied round the neck with ribbons (Fig. 17). It was used both as a sign that its wearer was on duty and also to indicate his rank as shown by the following Royal Warrant:

"1st Sept. 1684. Winchester.

"For the better distinction of our officers serving Us in Our companies of Foot, Our will and pleasure is that all Captains of Foot wear no other corselet than of the colour of gold, all Lieutenants black corselets studded with gold and the Ensigns corselets of silver."[1]

A Regimental Order issued to the Coldstream Regiment of Foot Guards for the Review by James II on Hounslow Heath, 30th June, 1686, directs that "the Colonel and other officers upon duty shall wear their gorgets."

Officers' waistcoats and gloves were often ornamented with gold or silver fringes. The beaver hats were bound with gold or silver lace and in some cases adorned with feathers. Sir James Turner in his *Pallas Armata*, written in 1670–71, says that the Captains wore plumes and the Lieutenants none.

[1] W.O. Papers, P.R.O., W.O. 26/6.

From the lists of clothing supplied to units it appears that the superior officers had gold lace and the subalterns silver.

Another point that strikes one is the vast quantity of buttons used in ornamenting the coats. According to one estimate the officers of Sir John Hanmer's regiment (later the 11th Foot) had sixty gilt buttons on their coats.

Sergeants and Corporals were distinguished by having the seams of their coats laced with silver of different widths and silver bands and edging to their hats. The Sergeants were armed with halberds, the Corporals in general carried muskets, except that those of the Foot Guards are described as carrying pole-axes.

Pikemen at the Restoration wore a buff coat, gloves, pot or helmet (Fig. 10), breast and back plates and possibly for a short time tassets (a series of overlapping narrow steel plates attached to the base of the cuirass to protect the thighs) (Fig. 8). The tassets seem soon to have been laid aside, but how long the cuirass and pot continued in use seems uncertain. Colonel Walton states that it was still in use after the arrival of William III. There are several representations of this period, however, which show the Pikes dressed in coats and hats like the rest of the battalion and without any defensive armour. It is probable that its continued use varied in different regiments.

FIG. 18. Pikeman, Foot Guards.
"Draw your Sword and order your Pike."

In the early years of Charles II's reign the Pikes in some regiments appear to have adopted a special uniform differing from the rest of the battalion. This in some cases was the regiment's colours reversed, i.e. a coat of the facing colour with red cuffs, in others a totally different uniform. For example, we find the Pikes of the 1st Foot Guards wearing silver coloured coats faced with light blue (Fig. 18), white sashes with blue fringes, and those of the Coldstream wearing green coats (Fig. 19), red cuffs, white sashes with green fringes,[1] the normal dress of the latter regiment at that time being red coats

[1] Cosmo, Duke of Tuscany, *Travels through England*.

faced green. The sash was a distinguishing feature of the Pikemen's dress.

His arms were the sixteen foot pike and a sword carried in a shoulder belt (after about 1686 in a waist belt). Although one does not come across any mention of Pikes on active service during the War of the Spanish Succession, they still appear to have been used at home for ceremonial purposes, as the colours captured at Blenheim were carried through London by the Pikes of the Foot Guards.

The military music of the period consisted of drums and hautboys for Foot and Dragoons, trumpets and kettledrums for Horse. It is uncertain if the fife was still in use.

FIG. 19. Pikeman, Foot Guards. "Order your Pike."

Fifes are shown in the engravings of Monk's funeral, 1670, with banners bearing the General's coat of arms attached to their instruments (Fig. 21). The drum major, drummers and fifers shown in the procession probably represent those of the Coldstream Guards, Monk's own regiment, which would undoubtedly be present (Figs. 20 and 21). Fifes appear again in Sandford's Coronation of James II. The difficulty here is to know if they are regimental musicians or those belonging to the personal household. Fortunately from the clothing bills in the Wardrobe Accounts we find that the Court musicians as well as those of the Household troops wore the Royal livery of scarlet faced with blue and laced with gold, so that these figures give quite a good idea of the dress of the latter. (Fig. 22) A bill of the year 1713 gives us the dress of a Drum Major of the 1st Foot Guards; crimson coat lined blue serge and trimmed with gold orris lace and gold twist between, embroidered back and front with Her Majesty's cypher and crown; sleeves faced with blue Genoa velvet, crimson breeches, a fine hat trimmed with gold lace and a band; crimson taffeta scarf trimmed with very deep and narrow gold fringes. Crimson cloak lined blue serge trimmed with broad gold orris lace before and behind and round the neck; the cape faced with blue Genoa velvet. Here we have what to all intent

D

is still the state dress of the Drum Majors of the Foot Guards after a period of over two hundred years, even to the gold fringed crimson sash. The Haut-

FIG. 20. Drum-Major, 1670.

boys had crimson coats lined blue and laced with broad and narrow gold orris lace, cuffs of blue, purple leather belts stitched and laced with gold, a "cordebeck" hat laced with gold and gold lace band and also a black velvet cap.

The Drummers seem to have followed the custom of the Pikes in having a coat of the facing colours, which was decorated with lace on the seams of sleeves and back and on the buttonholes (Fig. 23).

The Drummers' coats were further decorated by having the King's cypher and crown, or the Colonel's crest, embroidered on the breast and back. These occasionally had hanging sleeves, a peculiarity retained by Drummers for many years.

The Hautboys seem, at first, to have been dressed as the Muskeeter companies, but later adopted a style similar to the Drummers.

The following references in contemporary documents give some idea of the dress of the Drummers and Hautboys:

FIG. 21. Drums and Fife, 1670.

10th Foot. "A hautbois, blue coat lined red, with narrow silver lace down the seams, red breeches and stockings, a waist belt laced silver and a silver laced hat." (At this time the regt. wore blue coats.)

London Gazette, 1696.

13th Foot. "A drummer yellow coat laced, lined red."

FIG. 22. Musicians of the Foot Guards, 1688.

London Gazette, 1692.

Lord Castleton's regiment of Foot, 1693. "Drummers purple coats with
badges, grey breeches."

Clothing contract.

Coote's Regiment, 1692. "Hautbois, green lined orange, with 6 dozen
frogs and white metal buttons: the coats were embroidered
with badges and the seams decorated with orange
chains."

These must mean orange lace in some chain
pattern.

Farrington's or 29th. The drummers are already described in their
clothing contract, which mentions caps for the drummers
of grenadiers and hats for the remainder.

Lord Lucas' Regt. (34th), 1702. A drummer with a light bob wig and
light grey coat lined with red, crimson worsted loops;
white buttons, red breeches and waistcoat. A griffin's
head and a coronet, the Colonel's crest, was embroidered
on the back of the coat.

Note: The uniform of the regiment was red faced grey.

[27]

Fig. 23. Drummers, c. 1690.

Fig. 24. Hautbois.

The following appear to be the first orders for the training of men as Grenadiers:

19 May 1677. C.R.

Whereas We have thought fit that two soldiers of each company now in Town of the two Regiments of Our Foot Guards shall be trained and exercised by Our Trusty and well-beloved Captain Charles Lloyd for the duty of Grenadiers, Our will and pleasure is that out of the stores within the Office of Our Ordnance you caused to be delivered unto the said Captain Charles Lloyd:

34 Grenadier pouches
34 fuzees
34 Hatchets and girdles
34 bayonets

for the use of 34 soldiers in Colonel John Russel's regiment.

By His Majesty's command.

Williamson.

A   B   C   D   E

Fig. 25. Fur Caps.

The foregoing may mean there were to be two Grenadiers in each company, but it is more probable that the thirty-four men detached were formed into a Grenadier company.

By 1678 a Grenadier company was added to Infantry regiments and

FIG. 26. Grenadier, c. 1680.

was the exact shape of these first caps it is difficult to determine. Evelyn in his diary describes them at the review on Hounslow Heath:

"29th June 1678. Now were brought into service a new sort of soldiers called grenadiers who were dexterous in flinging hand grenades. Everyone having a pouch full. They had furred caps with coped crowns like Janizaries which made them look very fierce and some had long hoods hanging down behind as we picture fools. The clothing being like wise pie-bald yellow and red." (i.e. red faced with yellow.)

owing, it is said, to the necessity of having to sling their firelocks when handling their grenadoes, they were given a cap as being more convenient than the wide-brimmed hat.

The cap was on the lines of the old fisherman's or brewer's cap with the bag hanging down behind. It was first bound round with an edging of fur, but this gave place to cloth with a raised and stiffened front on which was embroidered the Sovereign's crown and cypher or the Colonel's crest, in the case of the Royal Scots a lions' head proper. At the back was a roundel of cloth embroidered with a grenade. What

FIG. 27. Grenadier Officer, 1st Foot Guards, James II

It is most probably on this description that Richard Cannon has based his reconstruction and Colonel Walton has followed suit by showing a rather tall fur cap, slightly narrowing towards the crown, something like a very tall Hussar busby with a red bag hanging down at the back.

So far the only representation of a cap (Fig. 25, D and E), at all similar to this is shown in a painting by Laguerre at Marlborough House, where some soldiers in blue coats are shown wearing fur caps. All other pictures of fur caps have a much lower band of fur, which is sometimes shown rather higher in front (Fig. 25, B and C). As regards the first cloth cap with its stiffened front, there again seem to have been various forms, the most usual being the so-called mitre shape but much lower than it eventually became. There is, however, a portrait of an officer of the Grenadier Company of the 1st Guards, James II, which shows a more square shaped frontlet (Fig. 27); this appears to be the only example of this form, except for a print of 1698 in the British Museum, showing William, Duke of Gloucester, as a child, wearing General officer's uniform and drilling a company of small boys dressed as grenadiers (Fig. 30). These wear caps with fronts very similar to that of the Grenadier officer of the 1st Guards; the crown part, however, seems flatter than the pointed shape usually seen.

Towards the end of Anne's reign the bag was stiffened so as to stand upright and had so become the well known mitre shape. A pack of Queen Anne playing cards in Colonel Crookshank's collection shows a company of Grenadiers with the high-pointed front, but fairly low at the back, possibly to represent the crown as unstiffened. They wear coats with looped buttonholes and cross belts. The Blenheim tapestries show Grenadier caps some with bag stiffened and others hanging down, the fronts being decorated with a grenade or cypher; sometimes the grenade is embroidered on the "little flap" (Fig. 28, C, D, E). A Grenadier of the Foot Guards has his ornamented with a star with many rays having in the centre a red St. George's cross within the Garter. This same design is shown on the caps of the Grenadiers of the Foot Guards in the Marlborough House paintings; here, however, the star has eight points (Fig. 43).

A fine specimen of one of these caps exists in the Dublin Museum (Fig. 29), which is stated to have belonged to Captain Parker of the Royal Irish Regiment of Foot, who served through the Marlborough campaigns. There is evidence that the fur cap also continued in use in some regiments during the

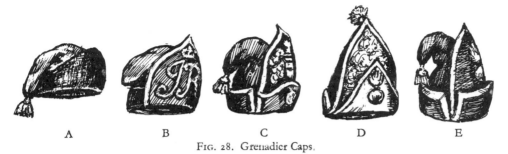

FIG. 28. Grenadier Caps.

Marlborough campaigns, as an advertisement in 1708 for deserters from Wynn's Regiment says one is wearing a fur cap and the rest one of cloth.

Grenadiers were also distinguished by having their coats ornamented with laced loops down the breast and on the pocket flaps. The laces often had one or two lines of colour worked into them and were tufted at the ends (Fig. 26). The famous old song "The British Grenadiers" gives an excellent description in the lines

"Who carry caps and pouches
And wear the loop-ed clothes."

In the paintings at Marlborough House the Foot Guards and some other infantry have their coats fitted with deep turndown collars of the facing colour. This is most unusual for the period; it appears again, however, on a

FIG. 29. Grenadier Cap. 18th Royal Irish Regiment.

[31]

Queen Anne screen in the collection of Colonel Crookshank. This has a battle scene (probably intended for Blenheim) painted on it, and shows some Grenadiers of the Guards dressed in exactly the same uniforms with blue turndown collars.

The equipment and arms of the Grenadier in 1678 consisted of a lighter type of firelock or fuzee, fitted with a broad leather sling, a grenade pouch on a shoulder belt, bayonets, cartouche boxes and girdles, and a hammer hatchet and girdle. This latter was for cutting down and clearing obstacles when

Fig. 30. The Duke of Gloucester and his company of boy Grenadiers.

attacking fortified positions. At times the hatchet was carried in a leather socket at the back of the grenado pouch (Fig. 31).

Swords were given to Grenadiers, but these are not mentioned in the early lists. In 1686 bayonets were issued to the musketeers of the two regiments of Foot Guards, the Grenadiers excepted.

The N.C.O.'s at first appear to have carried halberds, or partizans, as these are mentioned in the list of arms and equipment to be drawn from Ordnance in 1684. Later they carried firelocks, as did the officers. The cartouche boxes of the officers were often covered in velvet and richly embroidered with gold or silver (Fig. 48).

INFANTRY

Musketeers at the Restoration were equipped with the matchlock, **a** bandolier or collar of cartridges, which was sometimes called the **Twelve** Apostles, to which was attached the priming horn or flask, the bullet bag **and,**

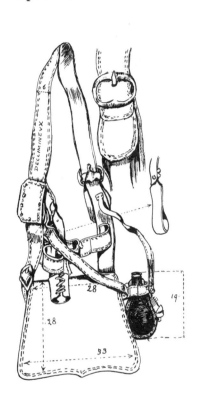

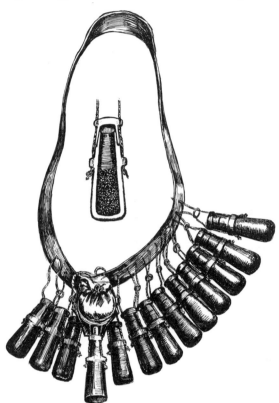

FIG. 31. Infantry equipment.   FIG. 32. Bandolier of cartridges.

when not in use, the slow match (Fig. 32), and finally a sword in a shoulder belt. The matchlock rest seems to have fallen into disuse during the Civil War.

In 1673 the Guards were equipped with bandoliers covered with red leather.

In 1660 General Monk ordered his regiment (later the Coldstream Guards) to return their matchlocks to Store and draw firelocks in their place. For some unexplained reason, however, this regiment was again armed with the first mentioned weapon. The proportion of firelocks and matchlocks per regiment continued to vary until the final disappearance of the latter (Fig. 33 A and 34).

The matchlock had many disadvantages, which are fully recorded by

[33]

the authors of military works of the time. It is emphasised that the match could not be kept burning in rainy weather, thus putting the piece out of action; that a certain amount of loose powder was spilt by the musketeer in handling his cartridge charges and priming flask, which was often set alight, exploding the whole of the ammunition on the bandolier and burning the man, or even worse in the case of musketeers refilling their bandoliers at the barrel of reserve powder during an action and exploding the contents by a spark from their slow match; that in night attacks the large number of lighted matches gave away the position to the enemy. On occasion, however, this fact was turned to advantage, as a number of matches were kept burning by a few musketeers, which convinced the enemy that an assault was intended from that direction, whereas, in the meantime, the real attack was launched on a totally different part of their line. Besides the wooden cartridges the bandolier had a small pouch or bullet bag, a reserve piece of match and a priming horn fastened to it. The priming horn contained powder of a finer grain for the touch hole. To avoid undoing the bullet bag, and thus save time, the musketeer seems to have placed several bullets in his mouth when in action. It was probably from this habit that it was one of the conditions of a fortress surrendering with the honours of war that the musketeers should march out with matches lighted and bullet in mouth (Figs. 33 B and 34).

With the advent of the flintlock, and the introduction of the cartridge containing bullet and charge, a great advance was made. To load his piece the musketeer bit off the paper end and, placing the whole cartridge in the barrel, the bullet end uppermost, he rammed down the whole charge, the paper wrapper and wad forming a pad over the charge. A priming horn was still used for many years.

The nomenclature of firelock seems to have included the snaphance and flintlock. The snaphance was the predecessor of the flintlock and was invented about the middle of the sixteenth century. Its mechanism was much simpler than that of the wheel-lock and therefore cheaper to manufacture. The wheel was replaced by a hammer striking against a piece of sulphurous pyrites and producing sparks which ignited the priming powder. It seems fairly certain that generally speaking the snaphance, so far as military equipment was concerned, merely meant a flintlock.

At the Coronation of James II in 1686 the musketeer companies of the Foot Guards were armed with snaphance muskets with sanguine barrels three

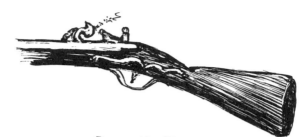

Reverse side of FIG. 33A.

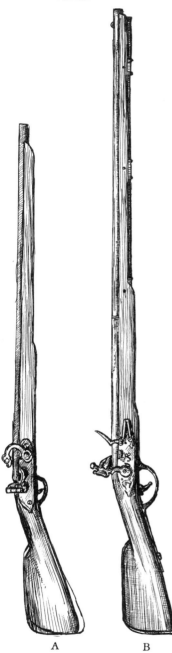

FIG. 34. Match lock.

FIG. 35. Flint lock, James II.

A   B

FIG. 33. (A) Match lock musket.
(B) Flint lock musket, James II.

feet eight inches long, but still retained the collar or bandolier of cartridges. The Grenadier companies on the same occasion are described as having long carbines strapt (i.e. furnished with a strap or sling) with barrels three feet two inches in length.

Grenadiers and Fusiliers were always armed with firelocks. These were provided with slings whilst those of musketeers had none.

The proportion of firelocks and matchlocks during the last campaigns of William III was about fifty per cent per company. The bandolier of cartridges remained in use to some extent until the end of the century in spite of the fact that in 1693 cartouche boxes were issued to most regiments.

The (7th) Royal Fusiliers were all armed with fuzils, a lighter type of firelock, even their officers carrying it instead of the half pike or partizan. They had no Pikes or Grenadier company, but had a miner company attached to it armed with carbines, cartouche boxes and hammer hatchets. They wore a cloth cap similar to that of the Grenadiers.

The bayonet, which had already existed as a hunting weapon in the sixteenth century was then adopted as a military arm in the French Army. It is often said that they were first issued to the Tangier regiment (now the Queen's Royal West Surrey Regiment), but on the 14th March, 1662, it was ordered "that the French Pikes, and the short swords or bayonettes that lately were received from Dunkirk be surveyed and an account presented to this office of their defects to the end a contract be made for their speedy repair," and on the 17th March, 1662 ordered "that the bayonettes lately received from Dunkirk be issued to the persons, to be by them made clean and repaired and returned within ten days space att 14$^{d.}$ a piece. Joseph

FIG. 36. Plug bayonet, James II.

Awdeley 200, Samuel Law 200 Robert Steadman 100."[1] It is possible that these had been manufactured and bought in France. In its early form of the plug bayonet (Fig. 36), it consisted of a steel blade with straight quillons or cross guards, fitted into a tapering wooden haft, which could be thrust into the muzzle of the musket. In this shape, it resembled a dagger and is so called

[1] P.R.O. Papers.

in the early drill manuals. With its appearance the shoulder belt was discarded and a waist belt with frogs for the sword and bayonet came into use. In 1673 the bayonet was issued to Infantry and Dragoons, but apparently fell into disuse until 1686, when it generally formed part of the equipment of Musketeer companies and the regiment of Fusiliers, Grenadiers having had it since their formation. By the end of the century most regiments were armed with it.

About 1690 it was found that the plug bayonet had the great disadvantage that once being fixed in the barrel it was impossible for the soldier to fire his piece, and another form was experimented with. This was the ring bayonet (Fig. 37, A and B). Here the blade was attached to two rings, which were slipped over the muzzle without blocking the barrel. This type is said to have been adopted by Major-General Mackay after the battle of Killiecrankie (27th of June, 1689).

This model seems also to have had its defects, as at a trial demonstration before Louis XIV many of the bayonets fell to the ground on the men firing. This may have been one of the reasons why in spite of some of its advantages over the plug bayonet the latter still remained in use even during the War of the Spanish Succession.

The ring bayonet seems to have varied in form in its initial stages. After the two rings, the blade was welded directly to a solid socket without any bracket-shaped curve (Fig. 37, C). In other examples instead of the dagger-shaped blade it was more in the shape of a javelin or dart, with a narrow haft and spear-shaped head. It finally took approximately the form it was to retain for about two centuries.

In 1662 a regiment was raised by beat of drum in England and entitled "Our Regiment of Guards in the Kingdom of Ireland." Thus it was originally composed of Englishmen. They were given twelve colours of crimson and yellow taffety with the King's badges "painted and guilded thereon." It is possible that this means the red cross of St. George on a yellow field. No details of their uniform have so far come to light, and although their ensigns were crimson and yellow it by no means follows that their coats were of the same colours, as it was the exception rather than the rule for them to match at this period.

Later James II replaced the English Protestants by Irish Catholics, and after the Treaty of Limerick one battalion followed him to France, where it eventually entered the service of the French monarch as Dorington's Regiment, its uniform then being red faced blue. It is curious to find that these Irish regiments followed the changes and details of dress peculiar to the English army up to the time of their final disappearance, long after they had ceased to be Irish except in name.

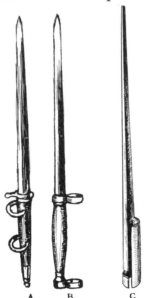
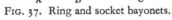

FIG. 37. Ring and socket bayonets.

FIG. 38. Cartouch box.

James II had been a gifted and industrious student of the military profession. He had served under the great Turenne and had studied the administrative organisation of Louvois, one of the greatest of War Ministers. It was undoubtedly due to his study of that Minister's system that James became such an able and efficient Quartermaster-General, whose administration did so much to improve the army. Wellington, on becoming Master-General of the Ordnance, declared that certain regulations with respect to that office, which had been introduced by James, had never since been improved on.

James took a justifiable pride that "he had formed a very complete body of men tho' not numerous, with the reputation of being the best paid, the best equipped and the most sightly troops of any in Europe." After his flight in 1688 and the occupation of the capital by William of Orange, one can understand that the Londoners remarked on the difference between the smart, well-dressed English soldiery and the slovenly appearance of the foreigners. Yet so unsettled was the state of the country, and such the disorganising effect on the army of the political upheaval, that not a year later the only troops in Schomberg's army in Ireland on whom he could depend were the Dutch, Huguenot and other foreign contingents.

FIG. 39. Dutch Foot Guards, 1691.

FIG. 40. Dutch colour.

In the same year, 1689, came complaints about the troops of the first expeditionary force of the Regular Army sent to the Continent; but here Marlborough soon changed the situation to such good effect that in its first action of Walcourt, August 1689, the English regiments took a brilliant part, Hodges' regiment (16th Foot) in particular, holding up the entire French force while falling back on the main body. The Prince of Waldeck, after the battle, gave full acknowledgment to the English troops for the victory and complimented the zeal shown by the officers in training their men to such good effect.

William brought to England with him his regiment of Dutch Guards, who took over the duties of guarding St. James's Palace. They arrived with a strength of 2,000 men divided into twenty-five companies, three of which were Grenadiers. They were taken on to the strength of the army and appear in the Great Wardrobe Accounts under the title of the 3rd Foot Guards, the Scots Guards at that time being still on the Scottish establishment.

The uniform in 1691, as shown in a drawing of that date in the Dutch War Office Library (Fig. 39), is a dark blue coat with orange yellow cuffs, waistcoat, breeches and stockings, orange being the colour reserved for the Dutch Guards. Their equipment is a bandolier, musket and brass-hilted sword carried in a shoulder belt. The officers wore orange sashes.[1]

Their colours are described in the Wardrobe Accounts, September 1691, as "6 colours of orange silk both sides painted alike with St. George's cross, star and garter and other trophies of war £72; 6 pairs of tassels of silk with gold cawles and fringe; the ensign staves with broad gilt heads and brass nails." Another entry describes the tassels as being orange and gold.

The regiment served at the Boyne, 1690, Steinkirk, 1692, Neerwinden, 1693, where it captured some of the enemy's cavalry standards, and the campaigns of 1694–5 and 6, including Namur. It returned to Holland, but served in the campaigns of the Spanish Succession and suffered terrible losses at Malplaquet due to the precipitate attack of the Prince of Orange, which also imperilled the success of the battle. The other Dutch regiments seem mostly to have worn grey coats with various coloured facings.

Besides his own regiments William brought over other contingents of foreign troops. A description of "The Prince of Orange's army" in 1688 mentions "200 negroes wearing embroidered caps with white furs and plumes of feathers, then followed 200 Finlanders in bearskin and black armour." These last Dr. de Wilde tells me would be a regiment of Dragoons raised in 1672 by Prince Frederick Casimir Duke of Courland. In 1676 William had became Colonel-in-Chief of the regiment, the Colonel commanding being Abraham Eppinger. The regiment was brought to England 860 strong and received the title of Dragoon Guards. They wore bearskin caps and, Dr. de Wilde thinks, dark grey coats. In the painting of the Landing of William III at Brixham 1689 are some very small figures of a troop of Horse dressed in a blackish-grey uniform with grey fur dragoon caps with very dark brown bags. They are preceded by a cornet in similar dress but with a felt hat and he carries a black standard. A trumpeter is seen dressed in a similar manner to the officer. The regiment served with the army in Ireland. What the negroes were it is difficult to say. They sound as if they were attendants or servants, but at the same time it appears doubtful that

---

[1] Narcissus Luttrell states that "the Dutch blew Guards are now ordered to be clothed in Red." 21 July, 1690.

FIG. 41. Types of Infantry, *c.* 1689.

so large a body of non-combatants would be brought over on a military expedition the successful result of which was by no means too certain. A similar body of negroes fantastically dressed in skins and feathers is described at one of the State ceremonies during the occupation of Tangier, but there the occasion and circumstances were very different.

The Danes were remarked on for being well disciplined and clothed, "having their arms as bright as silver, every man a coat or cloak such as the Dutch Guards wear and you shall not see a man with a hole in any part of his cloathing." The infantry wore green coats lined red, grey lined blue, and two regiments in blue lined red and white respectively. The Horse wore white with buff waistcoats.

Besides these, there were several regiments of French Huguenots, both Horse and Foot, some of which continued on the strength of the English army and served through the War of the Spanish Succession.

A picture of the soldier of those days as he appeared on parade can be gathered from a book entitled *The Compleat Gentleman Soldier or a Treatise of Military Discipline*, dedicated to the Duke of Ormonde "by an officer in the army." The date of publication is 1702, but the contents refer to a somewhat earlier period.

This book gives the manual for musket, pike and grenado exercises, and from it we find that some of the orders of our time were already in use. The remarks on general smartness, cleanliness and discipline might be of to-day, due allowance being made for the different style of wording. In it is the first mention of certain details not described elsewhere.

"Soldiers are to appear on Parade with their arms very clean and in good order. They are to have clean linen, clean shoes and stockings, their clothes whole and unspotted. Their hair or perriwigs tied up in bags, their hats briskly cockt, for nothing recommends a soldier more to his officer than decency and neatness of apparel."

To turn to the manual exercise, we read that the musket was "carried on the left shoulder with the left hand upon the butt end, the thumb about four inches lower than the hollow thereof, with the arm bended and joined close to your side, the lock turned upwards, so that the lower part of the butt end be right with the middle of your body."

On the order "Have a care of the exercise," the musketeers "are to draw off their right-hand gloves and put them in their fore pockets."

INFANTRY

In another line we read "The musketeer is to let his hand fall with a slap on his thigh." The order "As you were" also occurs, but this had already been in use in the time of Elizabeth.

The tactical unit of the infantry was the file, which consisted of six men, but with the gradual disappearance of the pike and the substitution of the musket and bayonet in its place it is probable that in action the depth of the infantry would not exceed three ranks. The practice of firing by platoons had not yet been adopted.

It has already been stated that the Colonel, as proprietor of his regiment, was responsible for its clothing and equipment. It is necessary here to say something of the pay of officers and men, as it will be found to have a close bearing on the supply of these items.

In the latter part of the 17th century the officer, having purchased his commission, had to pay percentages to the Secretary-at-War and to one of the other Secretaries of State as well as to the Chelsea Hospital.

His pay was divided into (1st) his subsistence money, which was a proportion of his full pay according to his rank and not subject to any stoppage, and (2nd) his arrears, which were paid yearly and from which the following deductions were made, viz.: Poundage, i.e. a shilling in the pound to the Paymaster-General, one day's pay to Chelsea Hospital, one day's pay to the Commissary-General of Musters, reduced in 1680 to one-third. On the top of these came various other means of reducing the pay, such as fees to the Commissaries of Musters, to the Auditors of the accounts of the Paymaster-General, fees to the Exchequer and Treasury and for the issue of pay warrants. Owing to the practice of keeping the pay of officers and men a year in arrears, the discount paid on its anticipation further reduced the sum. Officers on active service were often obliged to advance money for the supplies necessary for their existence and that of their men.

FIG. 42.
Sword and waist belt.

Turning to the men's pay, this was at the rate of 8d. a day or £12 13s. 4d. a year (for a Private); 6d. of this was set aside for his "subsistence," the remainder, £3 0s. 10d., was called "gross off reckonings," from which a deduction of 5 per cent or 12s. 2d. was made to the Paymaster-General and one day's pay for the Chelsea Hospital, reducing it to £2 8s., called "net off reckonings." This was taken over by the Colonel for clothing and equipment, which included belts and side-arms.

As can be imagined, this sum was totally insufficient for the purpose unless the Colonel was to make up the amount required from his own pocket. Various expedients were therefore resorted to, such as not reporting vacancies caused by death or desertion, but at the same time still drawing the pay, percentages, commissions and bribes from the contractors of clothing, etc., with the consequent result of poor materials supplied, at times even tampering with the soldiers' subsistence money on one excuse or another. All these were used to make up the required deficit.

The Captains of Companies followed the example of the Colonel, their chief source of funds being false returns made with the connivance of the unscrupulous Commissaries of Musters, vacancies in the ranks after a muster not being filled until a few days before the next and the pay being drawn in the interim.

The real source of all these irregularities was the corruption of the civilian Paymaster-General, who appears to have been free from all responsibility to anyone, and of the Secretary-at-War, besides the rascality of the commissaries, agents, clerks and others who had a free hand to enrich themselves by embezzling the pay of both officers and men. Later, during the campaigns in Flanders and Spain, another heavy drain was added to the officers' purses by the expenses of obtaining recruits for which the levy money granted was insufficient, besides which no allowance was made for losses from desertion or disease; this last was particularly the case with men cooped up on board the transports. So heavy was the mortality amongst the recruits destined for Spain, that the survivors on their arrival were said to have cost eight or nine pounds a head. It was the same with remounts, for which the purchase money per horse was inadequate, and losses incurred by epidemics or at sea were not reimbursed, nor was any allowance made for the expenses of transport.

The funds for widows' pensions were met by setting aside the pay of one fictitious man allowed per troop or company.

In Marlborough's army on the Continent the officers' widows were provided for by the voluntary contributions of the officers themselves. This

---

[1] Fortescue's *British Army*. and General Forbes *History of the Ordnance Services*.

scheme so appealed to the Government that they wished to include the widows of officers killed in the previous war.

This complicated system of pay, with its various deductions, percentages, etc., obliged the Colonel to employ at his own expense a clerk, known as the Colonel's agent, who performed the duties of regimental paymaster, and who by his fraudulent book-keeping, extortion and embezzlement was

FIG. 43. The Foot Guards at Blenheim.

able to convey a large proportion of the funds into his own pockets. It is not surprising that the plays of this period always represent the poor officer returned from the wars as being in a penniless state, having been mulcted of his pay.

The rotten system of the Pay Office had already produced a serious military crisis in William III's reign, and in 1702 the report on the books of the Paymaster-General brought about his dismissal for the misappropriation of Public money, and even gravely compromised the Secretary-at-War.

Marlborough took the greatest care that his men were well clothed and fed, and neglected no detail which was likely to contribute to this end. It was his foresight that arranged for the regular and proper supply of bread to be brought up at the end of the day's long marches to the Danube, and for depots of new shoes to be established so that his men should arrive in good health and well equipped. In 1705 he advised the bread contractors to use smaller wagons as being more suitable for getting the men's rations to them with the least delay along the roads of the Rhineland and the Moselle Valley. It was not likely that Marlborough would tolerate the chaotic and irregular way in which the pay, clothing and equipment of the army had been carried on. It was due to his administrative genius that these matters were put into good order and a proper system of inspection organised so that the men's pay was not tampered with and they received good clothes and accoutrements. With this view the Office of the Controller of Army Pay Accounts was created by Letters Patent, 1703. The subsistance money was to be paid to the N.C.O.'s and men regularly every week, and the balance over every two months. Stoppages for the Paymaster-General, Secretary-at-War, Commissaries and others were suppressed, and deductions from pay were limited to clothing and the Chelsea Hospital. The Office was to inspect all regimental accounts and muster rolls, to see that the cost of the arms issued by Ordnance were booked to the regiments who received them.

The Instructions read that "the General (Marlborough) having approved and sealed the patterns for clothing, the Colonels are to contract for its supply and exhibit to the Controllers the contracts, which must specify the qualities, quantities and prices of each particular. The Colonels or their agents are to exhibit to the Controllers the debt owing to off-reckonings on Feb. 24, 1703. In England the Controllers are to take care that the clothes for the army are furnished according to contract, abroad a certificate to this effect is to be rendered by the Captain-General or his deputy, and they are to see that the clothing does not exceed in cost the amount of 'off-reckonings.' Having satisfied themselves on these points, the Controllers are to certify the Paymaster, who in absence of this certificate, is not to part with the off-reckonings and where regiments are in debt they are to see that it is gradually reduced." This system remained in use for 150 years.

A Royal Warrant was issued on January 14th, 1707, and was the first charter to protect the soldier's interests. It is still the basis of the modern clothing and equipment regulations and is another example of Marlborough's admirable administration.

The main feature was the setting up of a Board of General Officers, themselves being Colonels of regiments. These were to supervise the supply of each individual Colonel. The patterns were to be kept in the office of the Controller of Army accounts in the Privy Gardens, Whitehall, where the Board met,

Fig. 44. Infantry 1712.

and with the Controller examined the proposed contracts to see if it was able to pay for what it ordered. After the clothing was made up it was inspected by three members of the Board, parcel by parcel, to see that it conformed to the pattern.

The plan adopted by the Board was as follows: Firms who obtained contracts submitted samples of what they were prepared to supply; these were compared with the regiment's sealed pattern. If found suitable these samples were sealed by three members of the Board besides the Office seal and returned to the contractor, who then made up the bulk of the order, which was examined by one or more members of the Board at the contractor's premises to see that it was up to the standard of the sealed pattern, but no Colonel was allowed to inspect the clothing for his own regiment.

1 P.R.O. Papers. W.O. 71/1.

FIG. 45. Sword hilts, c. 1706.

As regards equipment, swords, saddlery, etc., these were left to the Colonel to purchase as he considered best, and did not have to be inspected. They were repaired under regimental arrangements, and when worn out were replaced out of the off reckonings. In the infantry this was not such a big item, but in the case of the cavalry was a considerable expense.

The issue of clothing, etc., to Cavalry and Dragoons was called the "mounting", various smaller items supplied in the alternate years were called "half mountings". The infantry had an annual issue. Accoutrements, saddlery, etc., were replaced by the Colonel unless loss was caused by negligence, when the Captains became responsible.

Clothing for a Foot soldier, laid down by the Board of General Officers, 1708:

FIG. 46.
Sergeant of Royal Regiment, 1707.

"1st year a good full bod'd cloth coat well lined which may serve for a waistcoat the 2nd year, a waistcoat, pair of good kersey breeches, pair of good stockings, pair of good shoes, 2 neck cloths, good strong hat well laced.

"2nd year: a good cloth coat lined as first year, waistcoat made of former year's coat, Pr of strong new kersey breeches, pr of good strong stockings, pr of strong shoes, a good shirt and neck cloth and a good strong hat well laced."

From the above it would appear as if the waistcoats were always red, but there are instances of regiments having these garments of a different colour.

"The Sergts, Corporals, Drums, Trum-

FIG. 47. Types of Officers' coats, *c.* 1706.

peters and Hautboys to be clothed in the same manner as the soldiers, but everything to be better of its kind."

On one occasion an outbreak occurred on account of the extreme coarseness of the shirts, the men throwing them over the wall of the King's garden and shouting that they were Hanover shirts. "There being a great complaint among the soldiers of the 1st Regiment of Foot Guards about their clothing especially about their shirts, which were extream coarse, and it coming to the Duke of Marlborough's ears, his Grace immediately ordered the men to destroy these shirts; accordingly about 200 or 300 of them were burnt at Whitehall Gate on Monday night, and the Duke ordered the contractor to furnish them with better, he likewise ordered that they should have new blue waistcoats of a much better sort than what they had, the trimming

FIG. 48. Pouches and plug bayonet, *c.* 1706.

of their coats this said will be made much better."—*St. James's Post,* May 30th, 1715.

In Hollar's Tangier sketches we have seen what appears to have been

[49]

FIG. 49. Marlborough and Staff.

an attempt made to adopt clothing suitable to the climate. Later, August 18th, 1709, we find that the 38th Foot (now 1st Batt. South Staffordshire Regt.) for service in the West Indies was issued with the following clothing of a lighter description than that worn at home. "For each Private; a coat double breasted half way down, faced with yellow, but unlined; 2 waistcoats of Ticking or Ticken; 1 Pair of Ticken breeches; 1 pair of gaiters and garters, etc.: also a leather cap (in addition to a hat) with a little Peak which serves on occasion to drink out of."[1]

Ticken was a coarse material like that now used to cover mattresses; breeches and waistcoats of it are often mentioned in ships' slop clothing lists, and in these cases is further described as being striped. It is possible, therefore, that the 38th may have worn waistcoats striped with blue or red.

The leather cap is curious, as there is no picture showing a head-dress of this kind, with the possible exception of one figure in a set of water-colour drawings dated c. 1690 in Windsor Castle (Fig. 41, D). This bears a very

[1] List of clothing.

close resemblance to a cap which was worn by seamen, and appears in engravings of naval subjects up to about 1750. From its slightly uneven surface, it appears to have been made of supple leather or canvas painted or tarred, and has a small flap or peak in front, as described in the West Indies issue.

The file as the tactical unit had now disappeared, and the infantry when in action fought in three or even two ranks. The system of firing by platoons, which had been inaugurated by Gustavus Adolphus, was now adopted. This, together with the very high standard of discipline and fire control on which Marlborough always insisted, gave the British infantry their marked superiority over their opponents, who still fired by ranks. So great was the Duke's insistence on perfection of musketry training that he would have the regiments put through the platoon exercises under his own eye.

A new and improved pattern of flint-lock firing bullets, sixteen to the pound, was issued during Anne's reign. It may be said that Marlborough was the founder of the infantry which was to blast its way to so many victories by its steady and devastating fire.

A word as regards the men who formed the armies of the Duke. That a large percentage was drawn from the scum of the nation and the scourings of the gaols is undoubted, but in spite of this the general moral behaviour of the army was high, making due allowance for the epoch, and the men not only became good soldiers but left the army improved characters. This was due to the personality of Marlborough himself, who in spite of the general licentiousness of the period set a high example of conduct, which was followed by the rest of the army. There are no examples of his men getting out of hand as did Wellington's regiments at Badajos and elsewhere. Although, no doubt, Marlborough enforced the strictest discipline by means of the usual punishments of the time, his sympathy and care for the well-being of his troops earned for him their real affection and unbounded devotion and confidence. The memoirs of men who served through his campaigns all abound with references to the devotion of the men to "Corporal John" or the "old Corporal," as they affectionately called him.

Captain Parker of the 18th or Royal Irish Foot writes: "Each and every soldier under his grace's command being animated by his graceful presence and inviting example did in like manner, with heroic spirits and undaunted courage, unanimously fully imitate the steps of their leader."

Again, "the news of a battle (Oudenarde) was so agreeable to the army that all marched, from General Officers to private men, with all possible diligence, reciprocally encouraging one another to undergo the difficulties of the way." So great was the desire of the soldiers for action that several who were carried on horses and wagons before the fight, dismounted when the attack began and though weak and ill did very remarkable service.

Lediard says that "on the day of battle the Duke gave his orders with all the clearness and composedness imaginable, leading on his troops without the least hurry or perturbation and rallying those troops that were disordered without those harsh and severe reproaches which rather damp than animate a soldier's courage." This, Atkinson points out, is very far from Frederic II's "Dogs, would you live for ever?" and, it might be added, marks the difference of race.

Not even when the whole army thought that he was going to hurl them to certain destruction against the Ne Plus Ultra lines in 1712 did his men waver in their loyalty. And when instead he led them on the long night march which was to place them across Villars' much vaunted position practically without a shot being fired, and the order was issued that "the

INFANTRY

Duke desires the infantry to step out," they covered the forty miles, carrying 50 lb. of kit, in eighteen hours, though many fell by the way in their efforts to keep up.

When a factious Commons, aided by hired pamphleteers in their contemptible intrigues with Louis XIV, brought about the downfall of Marlborough and the cessation of hostilities in 1712, the news was received by officers and men with groans and curses and every symptom of rage and grief. The men wept and tore their clothes at being parted from their beloved leader; Parker in his diary "could not forbear giving him the precedence, it was allowed by all men, nay even by France itself, that he was more than a match for all the Generals of that nation. This he made appear beyond contradiction in the campaigns he made against them, during all which time it cannot be said that he ever slipped an opportunity of fighting when there was any probability of his coming at his enemy, and upon all occasions he concerted matters with so much judgment and forecast that he never fought a battle he did not gain nor laid siege to a town he did not take."[1]

[1] Sources: *Marlborough and the Rise of the British Army*, by C. T. Atkinson; *The Wars of Marlborough*, by Frank Tayler; Sir John Fortescue's *British Army; History of the Ordnance Services*, by General Forbes.

FIG. 50. Marlborough's Infantry.

[53]

MARINE REGIMENTS

1664–1713

It had been customary during the Commonwealth to send detachments of infantry aboard the fleet in the Dutch Wars, and this was continued during the reigns of Charles II and James II. The 1st Foot Guards, in particular had detachments in various ships of the fleet in these naval wars, Churchill himself serving with the King's Company. In remembrance of these services the band of the 3rd Battalion of the Grenadier Guards plays "Rule Britannia" on certain occasions.

Besides these detachments a regiment entitled "The Duke of York and Albany's, or Lord High Admiral's Maritime Regiment of Foot," was raised in 1664 "to be in readiness to be distributed with H.M.'s Fleet, prepared for sea service." It consisted of a Colonel, a Lt.-Colonel, a Major and 1,200 men divided into six companies, each having a Captain, a Lieutenant, an Ensign, a Drummer, 4 Sergeants, 4 Corporals and 200 men. In view of its special service it was to be armed entirely with firelocks.

Nathan Brooks describes it at the Review on Putney Heath, 1684, as being dressed in yellow coats faced red, red breeches and stockings and hats bound with gold coloured lace.

It served aboard the fleet during the Dutch Wars of 1669–1680. One Company was detached and formed part of one of the British regiments which served with Turenne. A Grenadier Company was added in 1678.

Its colours were as follows: "The Colonel's a plain yellow, Lt.-Colonel's, yellow with a red cross edged white, the Major's white with a red cross edged white and five gold rays issuing from the angles of the cross, the Captain's like the Major's but without any number or device. It is curious that there is no pile wavy for the Major's colours.

In 1685 the regiment became Prince George of Denmark's Regiment, and the uniform was changed to red coats lined yellow, dark grey breeches and white stockings. It was disbanded in 1689, many of the men being drafted into the 2nd Foot Guards.

MARINE REGIMENTS

In 1690 Torrington's and Pembroke's Regiments of Marines were raised. Luttrell in *Relation of State Affairs*, Vol. 2, p. 20, says "their clothes are to be blue lined with white and to have grenadier caps."

The regiment was to be all fuziliers, i.e. all were to be armed with firelocks and no pikes.

For the twelve Companies: "snaphance muskets, Dutch, 1896; bayonets with belts, 1896; cartouche boxes with girdles, 1896; halberts, 96; drums, 48. For the three Companies of Grenadiers, Dutch snaphance muskets, strapt, 474; bayonets with belts and frogs, 474; cartouche boxes, 474; grenade pouches, 474; hammer hatchets, 474; halberts, 24; drums, 12." In spite of the foregoing mention of blue clothing we find a deserter from Pembroke's regiment in 1690 described as wearing a red coat with blue loops, and another marine in a red coat with pewter buttons. A deserter from the 2nd Marines, 1694, wears a red coat lined green and a green waistcoat; so unless these deserters were wearing the uniforms of other regiments, they would appear to have had a blue as well as a red uniform.

Torrington's and Pembroke's Marines served at Beachy Head, 1690, and at the siege of Cork. The two regiments were amalgamated in 1698, and three more line regiments were converted into Marines, viz., Colonel Edward Dalton's, Colt's, William Seymour's, and Henry Mordaunt's. These regiments did not have a long existence and were shortly afterwards disbanded.

Officers of marine regiments were to exercise their men frequently at the great guns.

On June 1st, 1702, six regiments of Marines were ordered to be raised besides six other regiments for sea service. Colonel Field in his *Britain's Sea Soldiers* gives Luttrell's explanation of the difference between Marines and regiments for sea service, which appear to have been identical. "These last regiments were to serve not as marines but as land forces to make descents or otherwise as occasion requires."

The six Marine regiments were as follows: Colonel Thomas Saunderson's, later 30th Foot (1st Batt. East Lancs), Villiers', later 31st Foot (1st Batt. East Surreys), Fox's, later 32nd Foot (Duke of Cornwall's Light Infantry), Mordaunt's, Holt's and Shannon's; all these last three regiments were disbanded in 1713.

The six other regiments for sea service were to become the 6th, 19th, 20th, 34th, 35th and 36th regiments of Foot. The 4th, the Queen's Regiment, was also made Marines in 1703 and became a line regiment again in 1711.[1]

The uniform of the Marine regiments, according to R. Cannon, was "high crowned leather caps covered with cloth of the facing colour and ornamented with devices, the same as the caps worn by the grenadiers; red watermen's coats, buff waist belts, black pouches carried in front, with a bayonet attached, and buff gaiters." Cannon gives no authorities for this description, which very closely resembles the figures in the 1742 Clothing Book.

The leather cap sounds very like the leather caps lined with red which were worn by sailors at the time.

The following contemporary notices give further details of the uniform. Shannon's marines 1715 "found in a chest at Deal cutlasses and grenadier caps. The crest is a tyger's head on a yellow front." Lord Shannon's crest was a lion's head.

Villiers (31st Regt.), "deserter, red coat lined yellow."—*London Gazette*, 1702.

Colonel Fox's Marines (32nd Regt.), "deserters both with their clothes, viz., red lined green, pewter buttons."—*Postman*, 1704.

"A sergeant in his regimentals, being red lined and faced with light green and looped with silver lace, and another man in the same clothing but looped with white."—*Postman*, 1704–5.

Colonel Holt's Marines. "Deserters from the grenadier company with all their clothes, viz., red coats lined grey, waistcoats with loops of a mixture of red white and black, breeches and stockings grey. Grenadier caps.—*London Gazette*, 1702.

"A deserter with his regimental mounting, viz., red lined grey, grey waistcoat and breeches.—*Postman*, Oct. 20–22, 1702.

"—Grenadiers—red turned up with grey, brass buttons."—*London Gazette*, Dec. 25, 1704.

Several of these regiments, including Shannon's, Fox's and Villiers', took part in the capture (1704) and later in the defence of Gibraltar.[2]

Various Companies were detailed from the different regiments for the expedition which ended in the capture of Port Royal, afterwards renamed Annapolis Royal, in 1710.

These regiments were all disbanded at the Peace of Utrecht.

---

[1] *Britain's Sea Soldiers*, by Colonel C. Field. [2] *Idem*, by Colonel C. Field.

THE SCOTTISH ARMY

Let us now turn to the sister Kingdom of Scotland, which up to the union in 1707 had its own separate establishment.

Immediately after the Restoration the Scots army consisted of:

A troop of Life Guards, a second troop being raised in 1661, disbanded 1663; and a third raised in 1663–4 and disbanded 1676.

Lt.-General William Drummond's Regiment of Horse;

Five Independent Troops of Horse;

His Majesty's Foot Guards (Scots Guards);

Lt.-General Dayell's Regiment of Foot (disbanded 1667).

In the following years various independent troops of horse and companies of foot were raised to form the framework of a standing army, and were or could be regimented when the occasion arose.

Besides the foregoing, companies were also maintained as garrisons for the Castles of Edinburgh, Stirling, Dunbarton and the Bass.

There were also the Militia units of Horse and Foot.

As time went on further regiments were raised, including a "Foote Company of Highland Men," under the command of Colonel James Menzies. Concerning the actual uniform of the early Scottish regiments, little seems to have been recorded beyond that of the Life Guards. Still, there is a certain amount of fragmentary information which can be pieced together, so as to give at least some general idea of their dress.

The homespun cloth of natural wool, described as hodden grey in colour, was largely used for clothing the early regiments.

The Scots army of the Covenant, which assisted the Parliamentarians against Charles I at Marston Moor, was largely dressed in this colour, a flat round blue bonnet replacing the iron headpiece when not in action. As we shall see, the dragoons also wore grey before adopting the coat of red cloth imported from England. There is also a notice of providing part of the garrison of Edinburgh with "country cloth". It seems, however, that the use of "country cloth" had lead to the difficulty of distinguishing the Royal Troops from their adversaries; at any rate in 1684 the Privy Council asked the merchants and manufacturers if they could not supply the Forces, at short notice, "with sufficient cloathes at reasonable rates and of such dye as shall be thought fit to distinguish sojors from other skulking and vagrant persons, who have hitherto imitated the livery of the King's sojors, who agreed to import cloth from England of what dye should be designed." The upshot of the various meetings of the Council was that officers commanding Horse, Foot and Dragoons were allowed to import cloth from England: the colour of the cloth so imported to be red or scarlet.

For some reason, General Dayell objected to red being adopted by the Dragoons, and a fresh act was issued allowing grey cloth to be imported for the Dragoons, and red for the rest of the Army.

Captain Graham was authorized to import red cloth for the uniforms of the Guard of the City of Edinburgh.

Andrew Ross adds a little more by his reference to "Red and yellow, which were the adopted colours of the Stuarts from a very early period," and quotes from the accounts of the Lord High Treasurer of Scotland that "when King James VII (II) succeeded to the throne, he did his utmost to ensure uniformity in the clothing of the army, adopting invariably the family colours."

There are some notices which seem to refer to certain regiments being dressed in blue coats, but these appear to apply more to the Militia.

To sum up, the Scots army, like the English, wore grey or red until the last colour was finally adopted for the uniform of the Regular Army.

Before dealing with those regiments which still exist, we will give a brief summary of the early regiments of Foot which were disbanded. The Horse, Dragoons, and Train of Artillery will be found under the sections dealing with those branches of the Army.

Lt.-General Thomas Dalyell's Regiment, raised 1666, was present at Rullion Green 1666, and did duty guarding the coasts of Scotland against a Dutch attack in 1667. Disbanded in September the same year.

Lockhart's regiment, raised 1672 for service aboard the Fleet, disbanded 1674.

Monro's Regiment, raised 1674, disbanded 1676.

Lord James Douglas's Regiment, raised 1678, disbanded 1679.

Wauchope's Regiment, raised October 1688 and marched into England to oppose the forces of William of Orange. In 1689, was on active service in Holland. Was in Ireland from 1690 to 1694, when it was again in Holland until the end of the campaign, after which it remained in Scotland until 1701, when it returned to Holland and served throughout Marlborough's Campaigns, being disbanded at the Hague in 1717.

On the Estates of Scotland declaring for William and Mary in 1689, ten regiments were raised. Lord Leven's (25th), the Earl of

Fig. 51.
Standard of Lord Rollo's Troop of Horse.

Angus's (26th Cameronians), the Earl of Argyll's, Lord Bargeny's, Lord Blantyre's, the Earl of Glencairn's, the Laird of Grant's, Viscount Kenmure's, the Earl of Mar's and Lord Strathnaver's.

Bargeny's, Blantyre's and Mar's were disbanded in December 1689, and a new regiment raised under the colonelcy of Richard Cunningham; on his being posted to the Dragoons, Colonel John Buchan took command. The regiment sailed to Flanders in 1694 and served at the Siege of Namur, after which it returned to Scotland, and was disbanded, 1698.

Glencairn's regiment, embodied May 1689, formed the Garrison of Inverary, disbanded 1691.

Grant's regiment was raised in 1689 and continued a unit until 1690, when nine of its companies, with some of Glencairn's and other regiments, were formed into a regiment as a garrison for Inverlochy, under the command of Colonel John Hill, where it remained until disbanded, 1698.

Argyll's regiment, raised 1689, one of its companies taking part in the massacre of Glencoe, February 13th, 1692. The same year it was in garrison at Dixmude. In 1693, it took part in the attack on the lines of d'Otignies. Lord Lorne became Colonel in 1694. When Dixmude surrendered, the regiment tore their colours from the staff to prevent them falling into the hands of the enemy. The regiment was disbanded 1698. Like the other corps raised partly or wholly in the Highlands, at this period, it did not wear the Highland garb. The Black Watch was the first regular regiment to do so.

Strathnaver's Regiments. There were three regiments raised under this name. The first in 1689, to be disbanded 1690. On February 1st, 1693,

Strathnaver raised a second, which served in Flanders from 1694 to 1699, taking part in the siege of Namur. It returned to Scotland and in 1701 again embarked for Holland, John Lord Lorne becoming Colonel in 1702, John Marquess of Tullibardine succeeding to the command in 1707. The regiment took part in the battles of Oudenarde and Malplaquet, where forming part of the Prince of Orange's division, it suffered having losses including its Colonel amongst the killed. It was disbanded 1717 in Holland.

The third regiment was raised in 1702, by the Master of Strathnaver. It remained in Scotland until 1708, when it went to Flanders and served throughout the war, being disbanded in 1713.

Kenmure's Regiment. Embodied May 1689, and formed part of Mackay's army at Killcrankie where it was cut to pieces, losing nearly all its officers. When mustered afterwards at Stirling, only 300 unarmed men were present. Disbanded 1691.

Moncrief's regiment raised in 1689 by Sir James Moncrief, Bart., who was succeeded in 1694 by Colonel George Hamilton. It went to Flanders 1694, and served at Namur. Returned to Scotland and again went to Holland in 1701 and served throughout the war; and was disbanded in Holland, 1714.

Lord John Murray's regiment, later the Earl of Tullibardine's. Raised 1694, disbanded 1697. It was described as a strong regiment and well clothed. It was largely employed on guarding the Scottish coast.

In 1694 two regiments were raised and commanded by Sir William Douglas. One regiment served in Flanders; the other remaining at home and being disbanded 1697.

Colonel Robert Mackay also had the command of two regiments. The first served in Flanders and was present at the siege of Namur. The second remained in Scotland under the command of Colonel George McGill, and was disbanded 1697. One Company, however, being retained for some months longer as a garrison for Dunbarton. This regiment was entirely armed with firelocks.

Lindsay's regiment, raised in 1694 by Lord Lindsay, afterwards Earl of Crawford. It remained on home service in Scotland and was disbanded 1697. From the clothing bills preserved at the Register Office in Edinburgh, the following details of the uniform are obtained: "The private centinels were dressed in white coats and breeches, and red stockings for rolling." Grenadier's coats and breeches, the same as above, with the exception that their coats were ornamented with forty-five loops. The Sergeant's had stone grey cloth coats, red breeches and stockings.

The Drummers had red coats faced with blue and ornamented with blue lace. Their stockings and breeches were blue.

From the following numbers and prices of caps it appears the whole regiment wore grenadier caps, and not hats, as this last article is not mentioned:

748 Private centinels caps at 6s. each;
26 finer caps for Sergeants, 10s. each;
26 Drummers' caps faced with blue, at 6s. each;
Whereof one for the Drum-Major, to be finer than the rest, at 10s.;
56 grenadier caps at 8s. each.

The facing colour of the "Pie coat" is not mentioned, but from the foregoing it seems to have been white faced with red.

The regiment was supplied with both black and white cravats.

The equipment consisted of buff-pouch belts and waist belts with bayonets. The bayonets were to be one inch longer than the sealed pattern and to be brought from abroad. The grenadiers were furnished with axes.

The Earl of Mar's Regiment raised 1702. Alexander Grant became Colonel, in 1706 and in 1708 the regiment went to the continent and served throughout the war. In 1709 the officers petitioned that the regiment should have Scottish recruits sent out to it. Disbanded 1713.

MacCartney's regiment raised 1704 by Lt.-Colonel George MacCartney, of the Scots Guards. It served in Spain and took part in the battle of Almanza. Was reorganized in England and in 1706 went to Flanders. Disbanded 1713.

Ker's regiment raised 1706 by Lord Mark Ker. Present at Almanza, and afterwards reorganized in England and joined the army in Flanders 1709. Disbanded 1713.

H.M. Regiment of Scots Guards was originally raised in 1642, the original commission being still in existence, and was re-established in 1661.

An order of Charles II dated 1669 states that the regiment is to be dressed in red coats, lined white, and in the Lord High Treasurer's accounts (Scotland) 1678, the coats for the twenty Drummers are to be embroidered in gold, with his Majesty's name (probably the Cypher) and Crown.

1684 the camp at Hounslow. Red coats, white breeches and stockings.

1688 the advertisements for deserters, red coats faced white, and a Sergeant the same, but with broad silver laced hat.

A grenadier company was ordered to be added to the regiment in 1682.

According to a print of 1685, showing the ceremony of the opening of the Scots Parliament, the Captain is shown wearing a feathered hat, a waist sash tied on the right front. The front of his coat is ornamented with laced buttonholes on the right side only, and carries what appears to be a leading staff. The Sergeant wears a waist-sash knotted on the left side rather to the rear, has a bunch of ribbons in his hat, and carries a halbert decorated with a fringe, or tassel, below the axe blade (Fig. 52).

There seems to have been an idea of adding a Highland company to the regiment in 1681, but the plan does not seem to have materialized until 1704. It remained in Scotland carrying out the same duties as the other Highland companies. The company consisted of a Captain, two Lieutenants, two Sergeants, two Corporals, one Piper and fifty Centinels, all of them chosen Highlanders. They wore the Highland dress, and were armed with broadswords, targets, firelocks, pistols and dirks. This is said to be the first instance of a piper appearing on the official establishment of the regiment. Captains could still maintain a piper at their own expense if they wished.

This Highland company, unlike those attached to other regiments, was brought to London and was eventually incorporated with the regiment, probably only retaining its Highland garb for a short time. In 1707, the facings of the regiment were changed to blue, the uniform becoming more like that of the other two regiments of Foot Guards.

The Regiment now called the Royal Scots or Royal Regiment was formed in 1633 by order of Charles I, by Sir John Hepburn, from the remnants of his own and other Scottish regiments which had been serving in Sweden. It is from this date that the consecutive history of the regiment begins. It was taken into the pay of France under the title of the Regiment d'Hebron, the French corruption of the Colonel's name. Hepburn was eventually raised to the rank of Maréchal de France.

The regiment was recalled to England 1662 by Charles II, but returned to France the same year until 1670, when it again crossed the Channel to England and remained permanently in the pay of the British army.

Douglas, who succeeded to the Colonelcy, was killed at Steinkirk. The enemy having captured one of its colours in the retreat, Douglas returned

FIG. 52. Scots Foot Guards, 1685.

and recovered it, but fell mortally wounded. He managed, however, to throw the colour to his men across the hedge or fence they were defending.

The regimental march, "Dunbarton's Drums," which is played to this day, dates from the Colonelcy of Dunbarton, 1678 to 1684.

A seventeenth-century version of the music is still in existence.

[63]

While in the French service, the regiment was dressed in red, faced or lined with white, as is shown by a Pass 29, Oct. 1667, for twenty-four bales of red cloth with lining, coming from England for clothing the "regiment de Douglas."

Another Pass states that the lining was white.

1669 Red coats lined white, grey breeches and light grey stockings. Pikes white sashes with white fringes.

1684 The same, but in addition "the Grenadier caps lined white, with lion's face proper crowned." The lace-loops white, edged blue (Nathan Brook's list).

1689 The allied camp at Tillroy red coats lined white. The regiment had a piper belonging to the Colonel's company, and also a drum major is mentioned on its strength.

Pipers are shown in the Tangier paintings. They are dressed in the same uniform as the rank and file in red coats and wide-brimmed hats.

The present Royal Scots Fusiliers originated in 1677, from an independent company commanded by Charles, 5th Earl of Mar. It was ordered to be trained as Grenadiers and "to be instructed in all things belonging to the artillery, as gunnery, casting of hand grenadoes and fireworks."

A commission dated Sept. 23rd, 1678 appointed the Earl of Mar (then eighteen years old) as Colonel of a regiment of Foot raised in Scotland, the nucleus being the aforesaid independent company.

The following arms and equipment from the magazine in Edinburgh Castle were ordered to be delivered to it:

548 English muskets and as many bandoliers, and
272 pikes.

The regiment was dressed in red, faced the same colour, grey breeches and stockings, and was in consequence known as "The Earl of Mar's Grey Breeks."

1691 List of the Army in Flanders: "Red faced and lined the same colour, grey breeches and stockings." Allied camp at Tilleroy: "Red lined red."

The regiment served in Flanders at Walcourt, Namur, Steinkirk, Landen, Deinse.

THE SCOTTISH ARMY

Lord Leven's regiment (later the 25th, and now the King's Own Scottish Borderers).

Lord Leven came over to England with William of Orange, he had apparently already a regiment raised from his countrymen in Holland. In 1689, however, he raised a new regiment in Edinburgh for the defence of the city and the Lowland Borders against the Highlanders. It served at Killicrankie, Aughrim, Steinkirk, Landen and Namur.

The 26th, or Cameronian Regiment (now the 1st Battalion Cameronians—Scottish Rifles) was raised in 1689 by the Earl of Angus from an extreme sect of covenanters known as "Cameronians" (followers of a Dr. Richard Cameron, a well-known divine), with a strength of 1,200 men, 40 drums, 60 Corporals, 40 Sergeants. The officers being a Colonel, a Lt.-colonel, a Major, an Aid-Major, Surgeon and his mate, 20 Captains, 20 Lieutenants, 20 Ensigns. It was equipped from the magazine at Stirling with 400 pikes, 500 firelocks, powder ball and match, 40 halberts.

In 1691 a grenadier company is mentioned, being provided with "Pie coats, grenadier caps, patrontashes, and belts, grenadier's cap badges, and belts, 60 bayonets with slipones conform." This apparently means "ring bayonets."

The regiment served in Flanders under William III. There is only one reference to its uniform, that its facings were white, in *Some Account of the 26th or Cameronian Regiment*, published 1828.

INDEPENDENT HIGHLAND COMPANIES

In 1667 Charles II issued commissions for the raising of independent companies of Highlanders "for securing the Peace of the Highlands and to watch upon the Braes." Included in their duties was the prevention of blackmail. These companies were commanded by the Highland chieftains or leading gentry who appointed their own junior officers. These Commissions were renewed from time to time, until the end of the reign of James VII (II). The lists of equipment furnished to these companies in 1674–77 include the following items:

> 300 firelocks, 300 bayonets, 300 bandoliers;
>
> two pairs of colours; 4 drums, 8 extra firelocks;
>
> 4 blunderbusses; besides moulds for casting twelve bullets at a time, and moulds for the blunderbus bullets.

A company of thirty Highlanders under command of a Highland officer was attached to the four permanent Garrisons of Inverlochy, Killichumen, Bernera in Glenelg, and Ruthven of Badenoch. Their duties were to act as guides and scouts to the Regular Troops on their expeditions to the mountains, for the maintenance of law and order.

William III on his accession also raised independent companies, who carried on the same duties as before.

From 1693 onwards, it seems to have been customary to attach Highland companies to regular units, as we find them borne on the strength of George Hamilton's, Robert Mackay's, Moncrief's, Ferguson's, the Earl of Mar's (Royal Scots Fusiliers), and Lord Leven's (25th) Regiments. These companies do not appear to have served with the regiments, but remained on duty in the Highlands, and as regiments were disbanded or sent overseas, they were attached to other corps in Scotland.

The strength of the company attached to Ferguson's regiment, which may be taken as an example, was: a Captain, 2 Lieutenants, 3 Sergeants, 2 Corporals, 2 Drums, 1 Piper and 60 Centinels.

From the following, these companies do not appear to have worn any dress which could be called uniform:

INDEPENDENT HIGHLAND COMPANIES

"The Board of General Officers inspecting and regulating the cloathing of the army observe: There is a peculiar cloathing for the three Highland companies in North Britain, not at all military, but like the cloathing of the natives there, that they may the better discover any designs, or machinations, against the Government, or the country, which if it should thought fit to be continued, it is humbly proposed that some particular distinctions or instructions may be given therein, for allowing such cloathing for the future; consisting of Plaids, Tartan coats, Trousers (Trews), hose, pumps, bonnets, shirts, cravats, shoulder belts, broad belts, powder horns, with belts and measures and broad swords with basket hilts; with targets and pistols over and above for the Sergeants, and how the same may be viewed since they can only be provided in the Highland countries very remote from Edinburgh."—Privy Garden, Whitehall, February 21st, 1708–9.

The above agrees with the Highlanders depicted by Morier in his painting of Culloden, some of whom are shown in tartan jackets and trews, or belted plaids; also with contemporary portraits by Waitt and Michael Wright.

Sir Ludovic Grant of Grant, who brought out his clan on the Government side in the campaign against Dundee, ordered "600 of his men to appear in tartan coats, all of one colour and fashion." The colour in this instance is not mentioned, but in 1704 the Laird of Grant, ordered "all tenants and others to provide themselves with Highland coats, trews and short hose of red and green tartan set broad-springed," and in 1710 that "all gentlemen and commons to make all their plaids and tartan of red and green, and to appear under arms."

SCOTS REGIMENTS IN FOREIGN SERVICE

BESIDES those regiments actually forming part of the Scots army, there were many Scottish corps which served in the pay of foreign countries. Although perhaps not coming strictly within the scope of this work, they still ought to be included, as in spite of the fact of their being on foreign pay, they still clung tenaciously to their nationality, and maintained the right to fight under the flag of their own country. Besides this, some of the regiments eventually returned to the British service, while the remnants of others were absorbed by existing units. The Dutch Scots Brigade, for example, returned to Scotland to fight at Killiecrankie, and later served under Marlborough throughout his campaigns, to return finally to the British army in 1793 as the Scotch Brigade, or 94th Foot. It was disbanded on the reduction of the army in 1818.

In 1620 Sir Andrew Gray raised a regiment for the service of the Elector Palatine, who made it his Body Guard.

It was a soldier of this regiment who performed the exploit of swimming the Danube carrying his sword in his mouth; creeping unperceived through the Austrian camp, he seized Count Bucquoi and brought him back prisoner to the Prince of Orange.

In 1623, on Gray returning to Scotland, Captain John Hepburn took command of the regiment with which he took service in the army of Gustavus Adolphus, by whom he was held in the highest esteem. Hepburn on one occasion, with his own and two other Scottish regiments, held a position for two days against a Polish army of 30,000 men. The regiment took part in the battles of Girlinerwals, 1626, Dirschau, and the relief of Rügenwalde.

In 1633 Hepburn with his regiment took service under the French crown.

In 1626 Sir Donald Mackay raised a regiment for service in the Palatinate, afterwards, when in the service of Gustavus Adolphus, to be known as the "Invincible" regiment. This corps had, at first, a strength of 3,000 men divided into fifteen companies. Each of the companies had three drummers and three pipers. From the fact that it was partly recruited in the Highlands, some companies at least probably wore Highland dress, of belted plaid, or plaid and trews.

A German print of the period shows men of what is apparently this regiment in "tartan array," and states that "on emergency these men can march over seventy English miles."

Mackay next took service in the pay of Denmark. While in this country the regiment was requested to replace the Cross of St. Andrew by that of Denmark. To this Mackay's officers most vigorously objected, refusing to fight under any colours but their own. The dispute was subjected to King James, an action which gave great offence to the Danish monarch.

Four companies of the regiment defended Boitzenbourg against Tilly's army.

At the battle of Oldenburg, where the forces under the Duke of Saxe Weimar were compelled to surrender to the Imperialists under Tilly, the Reiters in the Danish army having been routed by the enemy's cavalry, galloped from the field to the landing place at Heiligenhaven with the intention of securing the boats there, and so be the first to escape. While they were thus occupied Mackay's regiment arrived on the scene, having fought so vigorous a rearguard action that they were the only force to escape surrender. The Scottish Foot were not the men to stand for any *Deutchland über alles* and the devil take the hindmost, so bringing their pikes to "the charge," they swept the Reiters into the sea, and embarking in the boats secured their retreat.

Mackay returned to Scotland for recruits and was raised to the peerage under the title of Lord Reay, February 16th, 1628.

In 1631 with Hepburn's, Lumsden's Musketeers and Stargate's regiments, it formed the famous "Green Brigade" which fought under Gustavus Adolphus.

It appears from enquiries made in the Swedish military archives that there is no mention that the regiment was then wearing any but the usual military dress of the period.

In 1572 Holland appealed to Scotland for help in their struggle against the Spaniards. At the time there was a famine in Edinburgh, and owing besides to the large number of disbanded soldiers in the vicinity, it was feared that disturbances might occur. To prevent this by giving employment to the soldiery, permission to recruit for service in Flanders and other countries was given by the Scottish Privy Council. These permits were continued without intermission for many years. It was largely due to these Scottish corps of mercenaries as well as those from England, that went over to Holland, that the Spanish Veterans of Spinola were swept out of that country in the series of actions from 1578 to 1605.

At this time the arm par excellence of the Scottish foot soldier was the

FIG. 53. Colours of Mackay's Regt.

pike, with which their regiments at that time were largely armed. W. Patten writing, it is true, some years earlier, in 1548, gives a long description of the Scottish Infantry, which no doubt had not changed its tactics much in the interval: "Hackbutters have they few or none—they come to the field well furnished all with jack and skull, dagger and buckler and swords all broad and thin, of exceeding good temper that as I never saw none so good, so I think it hard to devise the better.

"Here every man has his pike and a great kercher wrapped twice about his neck, not for cold but to prevent cutting, and in their array towards joining the enemy they cling and thrust so near in the forerank, shoulder to shoulder, together with their pikes in both hands, straight before them, and their followers in that order so hard at their backs laying their pikes over their foregoers' shoulders, that if they do assail undiscovered no force can well withstand them.

"Standing at defence they thrust their shoulders likewise so nigh together, the foreranks well nigh kneeling, stoop low before their fellows behind, holding their pikes with both hands and therewith in their left their bucklers, the one end of their pikes against the right foot and the other against the enemy breast-high, their followers crossing their pike points with them foreward, and theirs each with other, so might as space and place will suffer, through the whole ward, so thick that as easily shall a bare finger pierce through the skin of an angry hedgehog as any encounter the front of pikes."

SCOTS REGIMENTS IN FOREIGN SERVICE

"The stubborn spearman still made good
Their dark impenetrable wood
Each stepping where his comrade stood
The instant that he fell."

By their superiority over the hitherto "Invincible" Spanish infantry, the Scottish soldiers established the reputation of being the finest pikemen in Europe. The matchlock was soon added in larger proportions to the pike, and in 1689 one regiment was almost entirely armed and equipped as fusiliers.

In 1630 the Dutch Army seems to have fallen on evil days, the Scots Brigade, in particular, being much neglected. Through the influence of prominent burghers, Dutch, German and other foreign refugees were being posted as officers to the Brigade, with corresponding disastrous results, in the actions of 1675–76.

King William, in expressing his displeasure, asked Mackay why the Brigade had not shown the same valour as formerly. Mackay piqued in his turn, begged leave to observe that the corps, although called the Scots Brigade, was in reality a mixture of the deserters and outcasts of all nations, and that commissions had been given to Dutch, German and French, in preference to young Scots officers and cadets, who had therefore left the service, but if His Highness would dispose of the foreign officers and replace them with Scottish gentlemen of family and raise recruits in Scotland, he would answer for the corps being as good as ever before.

The Brigade carried colours with the Cross of St. Andrew, while drummers and pipers formed part of the establishment from the beginning.

Like the other Scots regiments raised for the service of foreign countries, the Brigade no doubt had a certain proportion of recruits from the north of Scotland, and who in the early years of its existence wore Highland garb, but most of the rank and file were possibly dressed in hodden grey or red coats, but from 1674 red would appear to have been established as the colour of their uniform.

The History of the Scots Brigade in Holland, by Col. Ferguson, gives the following curious piece of evidence of the uniform preserved in an old Dutch tradition: "It is said that before Major Ferguson's expedition to the Western Isles in 1690, the people of Eigg were warned of its coming by a man who had the gift of second sight, and that those who were taken prisoner testified to the accuracy of his description of the troops, as he saw them. Some being clad in red coats, some with white coats and grenadier caps, some armed with sword and pike and some with sword and musket.''

As the regiment was now dressed in red, one wonders if the white coats were the drummers?

Dr. F. G. de Wilde has most kindly supplied me with much valuable information concerning the dress of the Scots Brigade. From the following notes, obtained from memoirs, journals, army lists and clothing accounts, we learn that the Brigade was definitely first dressed in red, in 1674.

The list of the army in Flanders gives Mackay's regiment dressed in red coats, lined red. Ramsay's red, lined white.

In 1701 Murrays (ex Mackays) had white facings, as the regiment received white twill and red baize, together with 316 brass hilted swords.

The Brigade served at Killicrankie, Steinkirk, Landen, and throughout Marlborough's campaigns, taking part in the battles of Ramillies, Oudenarde and Malplaquet.

A certain amount of details of its uniform in these campaigns can be gathered from a long ballad entitled "The Remembrance or the Progress of Lord Portmore's Regiment, 1701 to 1709, all wrote by John Scot, a common soldier in the said regiment all these years." The whole poem can be found in *The History of the Scots Brigade in Holland*, Vol. III, pp. 307–577. John Scot tells how in 1701 new clothes were issued with a shoulder knot and Dutch arms. In 1703 new clothes with stockings, shoes and a new hat, 1705. Lord Dalrymple succeeded to the colonelcy and new "pie coats" of red faced with yellow, but without linings, fusilier caps with the fronts embroidered with two lions rampant, standing either side of a rock with the motto "Firm," the grenadiers having a grenade and gun well wrought in red and blue.

From this it sounds as if the whole regiment wore caps.

1706. The regiment was now commanded by Colonel Borthwick and the old caps handed in and harden or harn issued for lining the coats (Harden or harn was a coarse material made from flax or hemp).

1707. The regiment was commanded by General Hepburn, and new coats, vests or waistcoats, stockings and hats were supplied, and the regiment reviewed in its new clothing.

The Grenadiers' caps being ornamented with the new Colonel's arms and his motto "gratus esto," "white black red and green the chieffe colours seven with all their inferior mixtures."

"Of the knot of the union made by the Britons
  And a sheaf of arrowes the Hollanders arms
  And a Lyon as fierce as can be
  With a hand with a shable (short curved sword)
  And a horse at the amble
  And guns and grenades in several parts stands
  And pictures of shables of steel
  And on the farrat of each grenadier's cap
  Are letters from the Colonel's name
  An I and an H wrought throu other twice
  John Hepburn for to expreme."

Hepburn was killed at Malplaquet and the regiment came under the command of Brigadier Douglas, 1710.

1711. New clothing or mounting issued, new drums were also received and these Douglas had painted with his coat of arms.

"Now Brigadier Douglas paints on his drums the bloody heart under the crown and weapons of war with the points standing out about a broad circle all round."

G

APPENDIX

<small>Notes on Uniforms from various contemporary sources</small>

1st REGIMENT OF FOOT GUARDS

1661. Red coats, buff coats probably for pikes.

1669. Red coats turned up with light blue. The pikes, coats of silver colour turned up with light blue (which was the King's Livery).

1684. Red coats lined blue, blue breeches and stockings. White sashes with blue fringes for the pikes. Pikes, grey coats with sleeves faced with black velvet, the grey coat being an undress.

Sandford's description of the coronation of James II gives the following details: "The officers were exceedingly richly habited, some in coats of cloth of gold and others in crimson velvet embroidered or laced with gold or silver, but most in fine scarlet cloth buttoned down the breast and on the facings of his sleeves with silver plate. Their scarfs (which they wore about their wastes) were "either net work of gold or silver or crimson taffeta* richly fringed with gold or silver and their hats were adorned with tours of white feathers. The Captains were distinguished by corselets or gorgets of silver plate double gilt, the Lieutenants by corselets of steel polished and sanguined and studded with nails of gold and the Ensigns had their corselets of silver plate.

"The Private soldiers were all new clothed in coats of red broad cloth lined and faced with blew. Their hats were black laced about with silver, turned up and garnished with blew ribbands. Their breeches were blew broad cloth and their stockings of blew worsted.

"The Musketeers were armed with snaphance muskets with sanguine barrels 3 foot 8 inches in length, good swords in waist belts and collars of bandoliers and the Pikemen pikes 16 foot long each headed wuth a three square point of steel, good swords in broad shoulder belts wearing also about their wastes sashes or scarfs of white worsted fringed with blew.

---

* The crimson and gold sashes for state dress and crimson for full dress of to-day seem to be a survival of this.

APPENDIX: NOTES ON UNIFORMS

"The Grenadiers cloathed as the Musketeers but distinguished by caps of red cloth lined with blew shalloon and laced with silver galoon about the edges and on the frontlets of the said caps (which were very large and high) was embroidered the King's cypher and crown.

"Each of these Grenadiers was armed with a long carbine strapt, the barrel three foot 2 inches in length and a cartouch box bionet grenado pouch and a hammer hatchet.

"The regiment this day was commanded by Lt. Colonel John Strode (who appeared in a coat of cloth of gold richly embroidered with silver)."

2ND OR COLDSTREAM REGIMENT OF FOOT GUARDS

1669. The regiment of Monk, whose standard was green with 6 white balls and a red cross (probably the 6th Captain's colour) red jackets, green facings. Pikes in green faced red.

1684. Red coats lined green, red stockings and breeches, white sashes with green fringes.

1685. Sandford's "Coronation of James II." "Officers richly habited but differing in their embroideries laces and fringes, which were gold and their buttons gold thread, from the officers of the 1st Regt. of Foot Guards, which had theirs of silver. Gorgets and corselets as the officers of 1st Regt. and their hats were also adorned with tours of white feathers.

"The Private soldiers, viz: Musketeers, Pikemen and Grenadiers were in all points accoutred as the 1st Regt. of Guards and agreable to them in their clothing except their breeches which were of red broad cloth and their stockings of red worsted. Their hats were black turned up, laced about with gold galoon, in which they wore red ribbonds. The sashes or waist scarves of the Pikes were white worsted fringed on the sides and ends with red worsted. The Grenadiers had their caps lined and faced with blue shaloon and laced with gold galoon and embroidered on the frontlets with the King's cypher."

1705. A deserter "wearing a grey coat trimmed with blue, blue waistcoat, breeches all with brass buttons, dark coloured wig and hat with large scallop lace."

1712. Deserter with all his regimental cloathing being red lined blue and brass buttons. The waistcoat lined with yellow, a hat with yellow worsted lace.

2ND THE QUEEN'S REGIMENT

1686 red coats lined green, green breeches and white stockings. Had a Grenadier Company. Camp at Hounslow.

3RD THE HOLLAND REGIMENT (THE BUFFS)

1684 "red coats lined flesh colour. No grenadiers."
1686. Deserter, in "a blackish coat the sleeves faced red" (either a civilian garment or fatigue dress).
1686. Red lined with ash, ash-coloured breeches and stockings.
1688. 21–25 January, Deserters "from company of Grenadiers in the Holland Regiment, every of them hath a new red coat lin'd with a buff coloured lining, surtout sleeves, cross pockets with three scalops, large plain round pewter buttons. Breeches of the same colour as the coat lining."
1689. Tillroy Camp. "Red lined buff."

4TH HER ROYAL HIGHNESSES THE DUCHESS OF YORK AND ALBANY'S REGIMENT. THE 2ND TANGIER REGIMENT (THE KING'S OWN ROYAL REGIMENT [LANCASTER])

List of clothing sent to Tangier; hats, grenadier caps, pikemen's sashes, collars of bandoliers, cartouche boxes, grenade bags, match boxes, knapsacks, pikemen's, grenadiers' and Sergeants' swords. Clifford Walton gives yellow facings but mentions no authority.

7TH ROYAL REGIMENT OF FUZILEERS
1686 red lined yellow, grey breeches and stockings, brass buttons.
1689 Tillroy Camp, "Fuzileers red lined yellow."
1702–3. A deserter "red lined blue."

APPENDIX: NOTES ON UNIFORMS

8TH PRINCESS ANNE OF DENMARK'S REGIMENT
Red lined yellow.

9TH FRANCIS CORNWALL'S REGIMENT
1687 c. Red lined orange, grey breeches, white stockings. A deserter (in undress) grey coat lined black.

1692 (as Brigadier Stewart's Regiment). Officers blue coats lined blue with gold loops, gold laced hats; caps, pouches, cartouche boxes of crimson velvet embroidered with gold and silver for the Captains and 2 Lieutenants of Grenadiers.

10TH THE EARL OF BATH's REGIMENT
1686. Blue coats lined red, red breeches and stockings.

1687. A deserter, blue coat lined red with red and white loops, red breeches and stockings, had long and red whiskers.

11TH THE MARQUIS OF WORCESTER'S REGIMENT
1686. Red lined Tawney, tawney breeches and stockings.

Note: Tawney in this case seems to mean a crimson red tone.[1]

1692. Gilt buttons for the officers' coats.

1705. A deserter, "in his regimental cloathes that is a red coat lined, with yellow, loops."

1705–6. A deserter, a sergeant in a red coat laid down the seams with narrow gold edging, and the pockets and sleeves with a broad gold lace, a yellow waistcoat and breeches.

12TH THE DUKE OF NORFOLK'S REGIMENT
1686. Red coats lined white, blue breeches and stockings.

Colonel Wharton's Yorkshire men in red with blue vests. The camp at Chester.

13TH THE EARL OF HUNTINGTON'S REGIMENT
1686. Red lined yellow, yellow breeches and grey stockings.

1706. Deserters, white waistcoats and white ammunition breeches, two with short hair and one in fair wig.

---

[1] The dress of a deserter in 1687, viz. a red coat lined red, white stockings, and a grenadier cap edged white with the King's cypher, indicates that "tawney" in this case means a shade of red.

14TH

1688. Deserter in a red coat lined red: white neck cloths, grey hose.

15TH SIR WILLIAM CLIFTON'S REGIMENT

1687. A deserter, red coat lined red, white stockings and a grenadier cap edged with white with King's cypher.

1690. Officers' coats scarlet lined red "a red coat with plate buttons made up (as a pattern) 3 bearskins for the Colonel and 2 Captains" (? for Housings).

16TH COLONEL HODGES' REGIMENT

1689. Red lined red.

1691. List of regiments at Gerpines, red lined white. R. Cannon for 1688 gives red faced white, white breeches and waistcoats but gives no authorities.

17TH

1694. A deserter took away Lieut. Desbordes' buff coloured breeches.

1694. Surtouts provided.

1696. Surtouts, the clothing now worn.

LORD GEORGE HAMILTON'S INNISKILLING REGIMENT (later Colonel Abraham Creighton's) raised 1689, disbanded 1692.

1690. For Lt. Colonel Hodson's coat, fraize (frieze) 15 yards gold and silk twist, 6 dozen buttons, gold thread.

Captains' coats scarlet with silver loops, hats laced silver, silver buttons, pair of gloves, pike, powder pouch.

Lieutenants scarlet coats with silver loops and laced hats. Pikes.

Grenadier caps, 8 loops, pikes, drum badges.

1692 (Creighton's). Officers' coats scarlet lined scarlet shalloon, 120 oiled skins for waistcoats; gold and silver buttons, gold and silver lace fringe, beaver hats and castor hats, gold and silver loop lace, and hat bands, crimson breeches.

GUSTAVUS HAMILTON'S REGIMENT (said to have become later the 20th Foot).

1691. Officers' hats with gold edging and bands, silver for subaltern officers, scarlet coats lined scarlet and laced with gold for superior officers and silver for subalterns, buttons to match, grey worsted stockings. Blue surtout coats lined blue.

1692. Coats and surtouts as before, gloves laced gold and silver, 6 horses for the Colonel's own use.

1ST REGIMENT OF FOOT OF INNISKILLING

1689. Red coats, blue breeches, drummers' badges, hats grenadier caps, waistbelts; Sergeant coats breeches, waist belts and sashes. 42 blue coats for officers.

2ND AND 3RD REGIMENTS THE SAME

5,000 white surtout coats

10,000   ,,   ,,   ,,

Clothing sent to Ireland for above regiments.

20TH COLONEL JOHN NEWTON'S REGIMENT

1706–7. Red coats lined and faced white. Pewter buttons.

22ND SIR HENRY BELLASYSE'S REGIMENT

1692. Officers crimson coats lined crimson, gold lace and gold fringe. Silver and gold laced hats; grey waistcoats and breeches.

23RD (ROYAL WELCH FUZILIERS)

1689. Blue coats faced white, white stockings and breeches.

24TH

1689. Raised in Shropshire and wore à blue uniform.

LORD DROGHEDA'S REGIMENT

1689. A Welsh Regiment. Clothed in blue and white similar to the 23rd and was disbanded on the arrival of William of Orange.

LORD CASTLETON'S REGIMENT, raised 1689.

1689. Grey coats and stockings, purple facings, red breeches.—*London Gazette.*

1693. Grey coats and breeches, hats, grenadier caps. Clothing contract.

MONMOUTH'S REGIMENT

1679. Grey coats faced blue, the grenadiers having red loops.—*London Gazette*, 28th October.

LORD CUTTS' REGIMENT (raised on Dutch pay 1674, formerly Pembroke's), disbanded 1699.

1687. Red coats lined dove colour, loops black and white.

1691. Red coats lined buff baize, tin buttons, white woollen stockings, buff breeches. Grenadier caps. Officers' coats crimson lined crimson faced buff, white stockings. The dove or buff facings were really a warm yellowish grey colour called Isabelle.

LORD LISBURNE'S REGIMENT

1690. Blue coats faced orange.

LORD KINGSTON'S REGIMENT

1692. (Now Colonel Henry Rowe's). Officers, Surgeon and Quartermaster, coats crimson lined crimson, laced gold and silver, hats laced gold and silver, white worsted stockings.

INGOLDSBY'S REGIMENT

1689. Blue coats, red stockings.

ROSCOMMON'S REGIMENT

1689. Red coats.

DUKE OF BOLTON'S REGIMENT

1689. Blue coats.

MICHELBURNE'S REGIMENT

1691. 40 Officers' laced coats, 40 Officers' surtout coats, striped calico waistcoats with silver and gold buttons, crimson stockings, white stockings, laced hats, three beaver hats for the Field Officers. Pike heads and ferules for the leading pikes, 30 gorgets gilt with gold and silver, orange net sashes, gold and silver laced gloves, caps for grenadiers, 1 scarlet cloak, 4 sets of new housings and holster caps.

APPENDIX: NOTES ON UNIFORMS

1692. 140 yds. grey cloth, 44 yds. blue, 276 yds. shalloon for lining, grey coats faced blue.

COOTE'S REGIMENT

1692. Officers' coats crimson lined crimson and laced with silver, 13 sets of silver loops and buttons for Captains, 26 sets for the Subalterns. Coats for grenadiers looped, caps for grenadiers with two for the drummers.

COLONEL WM. NORTHCOTE'S REGIMENT

1694. "A Sergeant, a crimson coat faced green with silver lace down the seams and brass buttons." (*London Gazette*.)

33RD EARL OF HUNTINGDON'S REGIMENT

1702. A Corporal, red coat lined yellow, yellow breeches being the regiment's livery, with white stockings pawned his halbert and sword.

34TH LORD LUCAS'S REGIMENT

1702. The "new clothes being red lined with grey.

1703. Deserter "with all mounting being red lined white."

1703. Idem, a red coat trimmed white, grey waistcoat and breeches with sword and belt.

1703. Idem, red coat lined white, new carolina hat, yellow belt burnt with a L and a crown. Brass mounting to the sword marked with L upon the shell.

EARL OF INCHIQUIN'S REGIMENT (formerly Lovelace's, raised 1706, disbanded 1712).

1706. Officers' coats scarlet lined scarlet with gilt buttons.

THOMAS STANWIX'S REGIMENT

1707. Red coats lined yellow, brass buttons.

COLONEL BRETON'S REGIMENT

1705. Breeches of light willow green.

COLONEL KAIN'S REGIMENT

1711. Sergeant, red coat lined green and laced with silver on pockets and sleeves, silver laced belt.

1712. A deserter in scarlet breeches laced silver robbed his brother Sergeant.

COLONEL WYNN'S REGIMENT

1705. A red coat lined with yellow with yellow and blue loops, a yellow waistcoat, blue breeches.

1708. Deserters from Grenadier company went away in their regimentals, caps and hangers, one's cap was faced with bear's fur, the rest had new red cloth caps faced with yellow and a wolf's head wrought thereon. Their livery red lined and faced with yellow with blue and white loops.

FIG. 54. Life Guards, 1661.

CAVALRY

1660–1714

THE Cavalry, or Horse, as it was then called, at the Restoration would have been wearing a dress similar to that worn during the Civil War and Commonwealth.

The buff coat still formed part of their kit. This in course of time became shorter and closer fitting until it developed into the "vest" or waistcoat, the buff colour of which was often retained long after it had ceased to be of leather and was made of cloth.

In 1708 during the Spanish campaign Stanhope asked for buff coats instead of waistcoats and again in the same year he "wished the Colonels to give their men 'vests de boufles' (waistcoats) which would be better for the service."

Cuirasses and back plates were worn by regiments of Horse until 1697–8, when they were returned to store. The officers, however, appear to have retained theirs. They were either blackened or left bright according, no doubt, to circumstances or the taste of the commanding officer. The painting of armour was in practice as far back as the reign of Elizabeth and was recommended in the Civil War as a protection against rust while in the field.

FIG. 55.
Triple-barred helmet.

It is not clear to what extent the triple barred or lobster-tailed helmet (Fig. 55) remained in use, but in a contemporary painting of a

[83]

review of the garrison of Tangier in 1677 a mounted regiment is shown wearing black cuirasses and helmets and red coats. It is undoubtedly intended to represent the Tangier Horse, a regiment raised for service at that place and which is with us to-day as the 1st Royal Dragoons. The North British Dragoons in the early years of their existence wore a Pot, which is considered to have been a helmet of this type, but here the word Pot is misleading as iron "skulls" were also in use and were often described by the same term. (Fig. 56). These last were simply iron skull caps intended to be worn inside the crown of the felt hat as a protection against sword cuts and continued to be in use as late as the middle of the eighteenth century. When not in action the men often carried them on their saddle bows.

To return to the "lobster-tailed helmet"—although James II, Claverhouse,

FIG. 56. Skull.

Viscount Dundee and other General Officers wore helmets, there does not seem to be much definite evidence that they remained long in general use in the British Army although they still continued to be worn in the Bavarian and Austrian armies during the War of the Spanish Succession.

The arms of "Horse" were a pair of pistols with barrels 14 inches long and a sword carried in a shoulder belt, which was often laced with gold or silver. The officers, however, seem generally to have worn theirs in a waist belt.

The Life Guards carried carbines and these were issued to other regiments of Horse in 1677. These carbines do not appear to have differed much from the infantry musket except that they were shorter and lighter.

The 6th Dragoon Guards are stated by Richard Cannon to have been granted the title of Carabineers in 1690, but there seems to be no instance of their being so called at the time.

Cavalry boots were at first of a buffish or light brown supple leather, but were soon blackened and stiffened into the jack boot with wide rigid tops to prevent the knees from being crushed in mounted action and were called "Gambados."

Hollar's drawings of the Coronation procession of Charles II show detachments of the Life Guards which give a good idea of the early dress, the high-crowned and plumed beaver hat, the short scarlet coat, or rather jacket, laced with gold, the sleeves short and edged with loops of ribbon according to the fashion in vogue. The breeches are full and short and appear to reach just above the knee; these are also terminated with ribbon loops, which show just above the high supple boots. The sword is carried in a shoulder belt and a pair of pistols in the holsters. For defensive armour a cuirass seems to be indicated (Fig. 54).

In front of the Troop rides a Kettle-drummer followed by a rank of Trumpeters. Both Kettle-drummer and Trumpeters are dressed in the same way as the Troop, but are not wearing breast plates or carrying pistols. The Drum and Trumpet banners are embroidered with the crown and within the Garter a shield with the Royal coat of arms (Fig. 54). In 1685 the Trumpeters were ordered to be mounted on white horses on State occasions.

It is probable that this was their state dress as in Sir Edward Walker's *A circumstantial account of the Preparations for the Coronation of His Majesty King Charles II* they are described in a somewhat less ornate uniform.

"The King's Horse Guard all well mounted having buffe coates and with white armour, their horses furnished with hooses (being a short ffoot cloth) with red scarfes and plumes of red and white feathers. The Guards of H.R. Highness the Duke of Yorke commanded by Sir Charles Berkeley all having black armour red and white feathers and red scarfes, with belts of His Highnesse livery."

The armour would, of course, be the breast and back plates.

Besides the Life Guards there were other troops present at Charles II's coronation described as Gentlemen Volunteers from the fact that some of them were commanded by Cavalier officers who had served in the Royalist forces during the Civil War. They may have been troops formed of their relatives and tenants, much in the old feudal way.

Major General Brown's Troop in doublets of cloth of silver; some Gentlemen Volunteers in white doublets under Sir John Stawel; Colonel Sir John Robinson's Troop in buff coats with sleeves of cloth of silver and green scarves (these are said to be officers of the Artillery Company) a Troop in blue liveries laced with silver with red "colours" with silver fringes; a Troop with six trumpets and Pink colours fringed with silver together with 7 footmen in sea green and silver; a Troop under Northampton in grey and blue liveries, 4 Trumpeters and colours or standards of sky-blue fringed with silver and 30 footmen; Col. Gorings Troop in grey liveries, 6 Trumpeters, sky-blue

FIG. 57. Officer of Life Guards, *c.* 1670.

standards laced with silver. Finally five regiments of Army Horse in breast, back and head pieces.

Count Cosmo of Tuscany in his *Travels through England* in 1669 described the Life Guards as follows:

"The 1st or King's Troop composed of Gentlemen or Officers on half pay dressed in red jackets faced with blue richly ornamented with gold lace and wearing white feathers in their hats, was commanded by the Duke of Monmouth.

"The 2nd or Duke's (of York) Troop in red jackets faced with blue but without gold or white feathers.

"The 3rd or General's (Duke of Albermarle) dressed in like manner as the 2nd but wearing crimson ribbons in their hats in place of feathers."

A fine painting of Major General Randolph Egerton by Jan Wyck (Fig. 57) gives us a rare and interesting example of the dress of a cavalry officer of the period. Egerton, who served in the Life Guards from 1661 until his death in

1681, is depicted mounted on a grey Barb and wearing a scarlet coat with short sleeves terminating at the elbow with blue cuffs, and showing the gold embroidered sleeves of a buff undercoat of unusual length, as its skirts reach to the top of the jack boots. The coat besides being lined with blue has what appears to be a small cape of a dark colour reaching to the top of the shoulders; this is partly covered by the General's hair, which he is wearing long and brushed out. A crimson and silver sash is worn over the right shoulder and knotted on the left side. The housings, if any, are hidden by the coat skirts and only the holster caps are visible. These are red with an embroidered design. In the background helmeted cavalry are in action and two Trumpeters in scarlet coats and with scarlet trumpet banners are seen wearing the usual laced hat of the period. There was one detail which was at first dubious. This was the curious light blue of the facings having a faint greenish tone, possibly caused by age or varnish. At a second view of the picture the colour was definitely a light sky blue, a tone which appears in other portraits of the seventeenth and eighteenth centuries, where one would expect the colour to be a much darker blue.

In 1673 Horse Grenadiers were added to each Troop of Life Guards. These were not composed of gentlemen but were recruited in the ordinary way, and were in fact a troop of Dragoons, being equipped as such and performing the same duties. It is no doubt of these troops that Evelyn writes in his Diary, 5th December, 1683: "The King had now augmented his Guards with a new sort of Dragoons, who carried also grenadoes and were habited after the Polish manner, with long peaked caps very fierce and fantastical." The Polish manner refers to the coats as the same term was used in France, "a la Polaque" meaning a long skirted coat.

Their coats had laced buttonholes down the front with tufted ends, the lace being of different colours according to the Troop. The Troop consisted of 2 Lieutenants, 2 Sergeants, 2 Corporals, 4 Hautbois, 2 Drummers and 64 Grenadiers. It is to be noted that the two Junior Officers both ranked as Lieutenants instead of Lieutenant and Cornet as was the case of the Life Guard Troop. When the Grenadiers served dismounted the Lieutenants carried half pikes. Like the Dragoons the Horse Grenadiers had drummers and hautbois.

The arms for each Troop were 66 fuzees strapt (with slings) bayonettes, 66 grenado pouches and cartouche boxes, 2 partisans gilt for the Sergeants,

2 halberts for the Corporals, 2 drums, 66 grenado shells with fusees, a case of pistols per man and swords and waist belts.

On the 1st October, 1684 the King held a grand review on Putney Heath, the forces being under the command of the Earl of Craven. A list of the regiments taking part and a description of their uniforms and colours was published by Nathan Brooks the same year.

The following details of the three troops of Life Guards and their Horse Grenadiers are given:

"The King's own Troop commanded by His Grace Christopher Duke of Albemarle consists of 200 besides Officers; distinguished by their carbine

belts of velvet laced with gold and silver, by their red hooses and holster caps embroidered with the Royal cypher and crown and coated and cloaked in scarlet lined with blew.

"The Grenadiers of this Troop have blew loops tufted with yellow upon red coats lined blew; with Grenadier caps lined the same and a blew round mark on the outside, armed with bayonets and harquebuzes (Fig. 58).

FIG. 58.   Horse Grenadier, c. 1688

"The Queen's Troop distinguished by their carbine belts of green velvet laced gold: green hooses and holster caps embroidered with the same cypher and crown coated and cloaked as the King's Troop.

"The Grenadiers clad and armed as the King's differenc't by green loops with yellow tufts upon their coats.

"The Duke's Troop and Grenadiers as the Queen's only distinguish't by their carbine belts laced with silver upon yellow velvet: hooses and holster caps embroidered upon yellow with the same cypher and crown as the King's. The Grenadiers as the Kings differenc't by the coat loops of yellow upon their breasts."

CAVALRY

In 1692 the Colonel of the 2nd Troop ordered that it should be entirely remounted on black horses.

In 1699 the lace on the coats of the Life Guards which had been silver and gold was now ordered to be gold only.

The feathers which had originally adorned the hats of the Private Gentlemen and which had been laid aside for about twenty years were now reintroduced by order of the King, scarlet, white and green.

Fig. 59. Life Guards, c. 1690.

A review of the Life Guards by William III was held in Hyde Park and described in the *Post Boy* of 11th November, 1699:

"On thursday last three troops of Life Guards marched into Hyde Park and were drawn up under their respective commanding officers. His Grace the Duke of Ormond the Right Honble. the Earl of Rivers and the Right Hon. the Earl of Albemarle.

"His Majesty rid through all the ranks on a neat Barbary Horse, presented to him by the Dey of Algiers, then he ordered them to file off, to the end that he might take particular notice of each gentleman and his horse as they passed before him. First His Grace the Duke of Ormond and his officers followed by the gentlemen of his troop all mounted on black horses, in their

FIG. 60. Cavalryman cloaked, *c.* 1688.

scarlet coats richly laced with white feathers in their hats marched by the King and then the other troops, which were well mounted, also in their scarlet coats richly laced, having red and green feathers in their hats passed in review likewise. The holster caps and housings of all three troops were all covered with lace.''

The Life Guards originated from the Royalist gentlemen who followed Charles abroad. One troop, the Duke of York's, is mentioned as charging at the Battle of the Dunes in 1658.

A view of Whitehall by J. Kip, del Smith, shows the two mounted sentries of the Life Guards. Curiously enough the title is Whitehall in 1724 but from the dress of the figures it cannot be later than the time of William III. Kip was working in 1688 so it is certain that he made this engraving a considerable time previously to the date of its publication in 1724. This seems to be the earliest picture showing the mounted sentries.

There were also three Troops of Life Guards raised in Scotland in 1660–63.

These Troops had their origin in 1650, as a letter in the Scottish Naval and Military Museum shows that Charles II had a regiment of Scots Life Guards in that year, which fought at Worcester and after the battle some of the remnants accompanied him to France, to be reformed as one Troop at the Restoration. Thus the Life Guards of to-day can trace their origin back to the Scottish Troops of 1650 and the English Troop of *c.* 1658.

In 1698 the 1st Scots Troop wore scarlet coats lined white with white cuffs with buttons and buttonholes wrought with gold thread, a blue waistcoat with buttons and buttonholes like the coat, blue breeches, a gold laced hat with a hatband of one twist cord covered with gold going twice round the hat and tying in a knot with button loop and stays conform, a shoulder belt of Russian leather if obtainable within the Kingdom otherwise to be fine red neats leather all covered on the outward side with blue velvet and gold galoon round about the edges, brass buckles and keeper, carbine belt the same with swivel and keeper. A patrontash (cartridge pouch) covered with blue velvet and laced with gold, with a small waist belt of red leather and plain small buckle. Housings and holster caps of blue cloth with King's cypher and crown, the housings to be one inch broader and one inch deeper than the housings the Troop has at present and the holster caps half an inch deeper. The housings and holster caps to have a gold galloon round the edges, swords with brass handles and hilts laquered. Gauntlet gloves with stiff tops. Large stiff jack boots with fashionable spurs.

The Sub-Brigadiers as above except the carbine belt. The coats to be faced on the sleeves with scarlet and laced upon the sleeves, pockets and seams with a gold galoon, that upon the sleeves to be of the breadth of the galloon upon the belts, that on the seams to be half the breadth. In all 110 suits at £2,974 sterling.

In the Life Guards there were four gentlemen who, in 1679, are described as commanding as officers, but having no commissions they were called sub-Corporals and sub-Brigadiers.

Sir Francis Turner says Corporals were called Brigadiers in the Horse, as is still the case in the French cavalry to-day.

In 1700 the dress was practically the same except that the horse furniture was changed to scarlet and the waistcoats to a finer light mixed grey cloth. Besides these the following additional items are mentioned:

"110 cockades of black ribbon cut out at the end, with gilt brass tags."

"Gold agreements on both sides of the breast and back font and single to the other buttonholes, in place of working all single with gold twist."

The words "agreements" and "fonts" here used are French meaning loops and the slit in the skirt at the back of the coat.

For the Sub-Brigadiers coats as before waistcoats with gold agreements, housings and holster caps larger and double laced. Shoulder belts laced with gold. 106 surtout coats for Troop of blue lined white, double breasted, faced on the breast with blue cloth with cloth buttons and buttonholes.

4 coats of finer cloth lined blue serge with silk buttons and button-holes.

5 coats of blue cloth lined and breasted as above with gilt buttons and faced in the sleeves with white cloth.

A troop of Horse Grenadier Guards was formed in 1702.

Besides the above Scots Household Troops and the Royal Scots Dragoons there were other mounted Scottish Corps. These were originally

FIG. 61. Scots Life Guards, 1685

raised as independent troops, which eventually were united into regiments.

Graham's of Claverhouse, or the Royal Regiment of Horse, was formed from various independent troops raised between 1678 and 1683. From the lists of accoutrements issued to the regiment we learn that it was equipped with head, back and front pieces, pistols, holsters, carbines with belts and swords. As the head-piece worn by Claverhouse himself was of the barred or lobster tail type it is possible that the regiment wore this helmet.

In 1685 the King to show his appreciation of Colonel Graham's regiment ordered that it was "in future to be Our Own Regiment of Horse and to have rank and precedency accordingly and the Trumpeters of the several Troops and the Kettle Drummers of that regiment to be in future in Our own livery and that there be in addition of a chryurgeon and his mate, also a farrier to every troupe thereof."[1]

In 1685 a licence dated 3 Feb. was granted to import cloth from England for the regiment and from this it is clear that the regiment was dressed in red coats lined and faced with yellow (the Stuart colours).[2]

Several independent Troops of Horse, which had been raised some time previously and remained on this basis until 1691, were then formed into two regiments of Dragoons known as Colonel Richard Cunningham's and Lord Newbattle's. Although changed to dragoons they appear to have remained armed and equipped as heavy cavalry. They were dressed in scarlet coats.[2]

Cunningham's regiment served in Ireland and fought at Aughrim, and served with William III in Flanders. In 1696 it became Jedburgh's Dragoons

[1] Ref.: King's letter to the Treasury 21 Dec., 1685.
[2] *Old Scottish Colours*, by Ross.

and returning home remained on the Scottish establishment and was known by the names of various Colonels; 1703 Lothians'; 1707 Lord Polwarth's; 1709 Ker's. In 1711 it was again serving in the Low Countries and was disbanded 1714. It was revived by George I and fought at Sheriffmuir. From 1715 to 1745 more English officers were posted to it until it finally lost its Scottish connection and became the 7th Dragoons (later 7th Queen's Own Hussars).[1]

Lord Newbattle's Dragoons, later Lord Jedburgh's until 1697 when Jedburgh transferred to Cunningham's. It then became Forbes'. It was disbanded 1697.[2]

Carmichael's Dragoons raised 29th March, 1694. It remained in Scotland and was disbanded 1698. The equipment issued included fyrelockes, patrontasches and halberts.[3]

Hyndford's Dragoons raised 1702 by the Earl of Hyndford, the same man who, as Lord Carmichael raised the earlier regiment of that name. His son James Lord Carmichael succeeded to the Colonelcy in 1706 and this regiment became known as Carmichael's. Disbanded in 1713 having again become known as Hyndford's.[4]

Cardross's Dragoons raised 1689 and disbanded December, 1690, armed with firelocks or fusils slung over the shoulder with a belt, swords and bayonets, patrontasches of leather and white iron, buckets and swords. The belts are described as being of a dun buff colour.[5]

Regiments of Horse wore crimson coats with regimental facings and cloaks of red cloth. The troopers as well as the officers often wore sashes, generally of red, but white in the case of Arran's Horse (4th D.G.'s) but this custom had probably died out by the end of the seventeenth century.

Colonel Clifford Walton says he believed Schomberg's Horse (7th D.G.'s) were first dressed in a blue uniform lined white and in support of this quotes the letter of a Major in the regiment in 1689, the writer saying "there had been a riot and that the Corporation asserted that it was caused by the officers and soldiers and that the blue coats came down with their carbines and created a riot."

[1] *Military History of Perthshire*, by the Marchioness of Tullibardine.
[2] *Idem*, by the Marchioness of Tullibardine.
[3] *Old Scottish Colours*, by Ross.
[4] *Military History of Perthshire*, by the Marchioness of Tullibardine.
[5] *Old Scottish Colours*, by Ross.

The cavalry, like the infantry, seem to have had an undress grey coat or surtout as an advertisement for deserters 1690 Schomberg's Horse (7th D.G.'s) mentions besides a red coat lined white with pewter buttons, a grey coat lined, with black buttons.

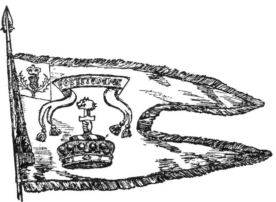

FIG. 62. Guidon of Cardross's Dragoons, 1689–1690.

The cavalry in Hollar's Tangier sketches are also shown wearing grey as well as red coats. The grey was probably their service or undress kit. The painting of the Review at Tangier represents this regiment in red coats with red cloaks rolled, and strapped behind their saddles.

A race meeting was held on Datchet Meads in 1684 at which Charles II, the Duke of York and the Duke of Monmouth were present. Francis Barlow made a picture of the scene as well as an etching. A cavalry escort is shown wearing buffish grey coats, buff cross belts and black hats, one of which has a small white feather or bow of ribbon. The officer is dressed in the same coloured coat and wearing a shoulder sword belt and blue sash round the waist. His hat has a knot or bow of red ribbon, and he wears high buff boots, the troopers having the same of black leather.

The hat followed the same development as that worn by the infantry and was bound with silver or gold lace. In the next century a loop and button are sometimes shown. Hats at times had the brim rolled over at the back and at others were worn with the point at the back. This was common to both Horse and Foot (Fig. 15).

The hats of the officers were often adorned with feathers. These at first were similar to those shown in the drawing of the Life Guards, worn round the crown with the ends showing over the brim; later, however, when the hat had become looped up on the three sides, it looks more as if the feather was bound round the inside edges of the brim.

Black cockades begin to be mentioned in 1700. It has always been considered that the black cockade was a Hanoverian emblem, but from the above this is evidently not the case. What seems more probable is that the

Jacobites having adopted a white cockade in the "45" the black came to be regarded as the badge of the Hanoverians.

The black cockade was also worn by many French regiments including the Gardes françaises, some even retaining it up to the Revolution. The

FIG. 63. Colonel of Horse (7th D.G's) 1688–1690.

white was also worn by other units, but this was in no wise regarded as a national distinction.

The coat, which was single-breasted, eventually had wide deep skirts with several pleats with rows of buttons on each side, no doubt so that it could be spread out when the wearer was mounted and thus protect the thighs against the weather. The cuffs were of the regiment's facing colour, and by about 1700 were occasionally edged with lace, the buttonholes having laced loops, altogether a simple and serviceable garment. It does not seem to have had any collar, although later on in Stanhope's Spanish campaign we read of the Royal Dragoons fitting a blue one to their coats. The throat was protected by a white neck cloth.

It became the fashion for officers to have various items of their dress ornamented with gold or silver fringes; this applied not only to their sashes but also to their gloves and waistcoats.

Their coats were generally laced down the seams and round the cuffs with silver or gold, the buttonholes ornamented with loops of the same.

FIG. 64. Dutch Life Guards, 1691.

The orders issued in 1686 by the Earl of Oxford to the Horse Guards (Blues) are of exceptional interest as they give one of the few examples of early rank distinctions.

All Captains' coats were to be of blue cloth faced with the same, the lace of said coats must be of gold laid double upon every seam and slits, with gold foot between the two laces, the buttons of gold thread with a gold thread round the sleeves, under which must be laid the same gold lace as down the seams.

All Lieutenants and Cornets must be the same as the Captains only a single lace on each seam, slits and sleeves, the fringe excepted.

The Quartermaster—coats must be the same cloth as the rest of the officers with a gold edging down before, at the pockets, slits and round the sleeves as the Lieutenants and Cornets, and gold buttons as the rest of the officers.

CAVALRY

The pockets of all coats must be of the same fashion, viz: two long slits on each side.

Every officer must have a black hat edged with gold lace and with a white feather. The trimming of the hats must be yellow as also the cravat strings.

This custom of distinguishing superior rank by an extra lace was also in existence in the French army, and is to be noticed in prints of the period, the cuffs having one or two laces going round according to the status of the wearer.

Besides his regiment of Foot Guards already described William III was accompanied from Holland by two regiments of cavalry, the Gardes du Corps, or Life Guards, and the Gardes te Paard, or Horse Guards. The Gardes du Corps came to England 197 horses strong.

Their uniform, from an official description, was a crimson coat with dark blue facings and linings, buff waistcoats, black felt hats bound with gold lace and white feathers, housings and holster caps dark blue. They were mounted on grey horses, which they are said to have handed over to the Scots Greys on their return to Holland. A coloured print

FIG. 65. The 4th Troop of Life Guards, c. 1692.

of 1691 shows red coats of brighter colour than the crimson housings and holster caps. The officer is wearing a dark blue sash round the waist and has white feathers in his hat, the troopers having none. A trumpeter is shown in a red coat with gold laced button-holes, long hanging sleeves with gold lace rings, his hat is furnished with two feathers, one of red and white and the other white and blue; he carries a brass trumpet with a blue banner (Fig. 64).

The portrait of William III at Kensington Palace also shows these

FIG. 66. Dutch Horse Guards, *c.* 1691.

Guards on grey horses in the background, wearing a similar uniform. The officer's red coat, however, has bands of lace laid on in rings up the sleeves.

The blue holster caps are embroidered with what appears to be a star.

The troopers have red sword and carbine belts laced with gold, and some have white plumes in their hats. The housings are blue laced with gold (Fig. 65). The regiment served in Ireland and at the battle of Neerwinden.

The Gardes te Paard, or Horse Guards, came to England with a horse strength of 480 horses. They were commanded by Hans William Bentinck, who in 1689 became Duke of Portland.

The uniform was a blue coat with the King's cypher and arms on the breast and back. A print of the battle of the Boyne by Romyn de Hooge shows the King's cypher and crown on the loose hanging sleeve.

The picture at Kensington Palace shows a detachment of Horse evidently intended for this regiment. They are dressed in blue coats with about eight gold loops down the front but no cypher is shown (Fig. 65). The cuffs are also blue edged with gold lace. The hats are buff-coloured and laced with gold. The holster caps are red (Fig. 66).

The Kettle Drummer and Trumpeters of the Dutch Life Guards wore the

CAVALRY

Royal livery like the other Troops. The following description appears in the Wardrobe Accounts:

"Crimson velvet coats trimmed with silk and silver lace, broad and narrow gold and silver lace, with gold twist between. Their Majesties' cyphers on the back and breast, leather belts ornamented with gold and silver orris, a hat with gold and silver lace and a black velvet cap. Cloak of crimson cloth lined blue and trimmed gold and silver orris." (Fig. 66).

The Troop appears to have had its Horse Grenadiers.

The Trumpet and Kettle Drum banners were embroidered with the Royal arms and supporters. The colour of the damask is not mentioned but was probably blue, the same as the standards.

The standards of the Dutch Life Guards now numbered the 4th Troop, are described in the Great Wardrobe Accounts in the following entries:

"1689. 6⅝ ells of blue Genoa damask for two standards."

"1689. Oct. For richly embroidering 2 standards with Their Majesties' cyphers and crown on both sides £30," and again
"2 colours of blue damask trimmed with gold and silver fringe and large strings and tassels (embroidered as above). Standard staves with belts and boot leathers."

Marlborough, who excelled as a Cavalry commander, was justly proud of his mounted regiments and took the greatest care over their training and equipment. He insisted on their being mounted on English horses and refused to entertain the proposal of buying remounts in Hamburg, as he had "always been of the opinion that English horses, as well as English men are better than can be found anywhere else." What exactly was the type of our cavalry mount at this period it is hard to say, but judging by the paintings of the time they appear to have been strong, sturdy animals with high crests and small heads, but lighter and more active than the heavy war horse of mediæval times. This was no doubt the result of a mixture of imported breeds, mostly Barbs, or with the Barb strain, crossed with English horses, which had been in progress for some time. The latter were likely to have been cob-like animals of about 14 hands. It has been stated that Cromwell's Troopers, who were largely recruited from the yeoman class, made long treks on horses of this type. Major Lamb in his *Story of the Horse* says that there were many Barb and Turkish horses used during the Civil War. It was this strain which gave the small head so characteristic in the paintings of horses of the time, and it was also, no doubt, an artistic convention to give the appearance of a blood horse.

The cavalry proper were mostly mounted on black horses, those of the

FIG. 67. Life Guard, c. 1712.

Dragoons being the smaller cob-like animal of various colours. The purchase price allowed for a cavalry horse was £12, which it appears, however, was not sufficient for the English bred animal which Marlborough insisted on. The cavalry in Spain bought their remounts in Ireland at £5 each and these are described as good squat dragoon horses.

The tails are always shown full and long, but the practice of docking had already been in existence. Mrs. Christian Davies mentions docking a horse's tail during the Marlborough campaigns. From the extreme shortness of the ears in some pictures, these appear to have been clipped, no doubt to lessen the risk of being slashed in a melée.

The English cavalry on its way to the Danube, in spite of the long marches and heavy going over rough country and the bad roads of that time, still retained its smart appearance with horses and equipment in such good condition as to draw forth the admiration of Prince Eugène, who was inspecting them in the presence of Marlborough. "My Lord, I never saw better horses, better clothes, finer belts and accoutrements, yet all these may be had for money, but there is a spirit in the looks of your men which I never saw in my life."[1]

The Duke was a great advocate of shock action and would allow the horse "but three charges of powder and ball to each man for a campaign and that only for guarding their horses when at grass, and not to be made use of in action."

He maintained that the sword was the arm of the British cavalry. In this he was following the principles of the dashing Prince Rupert, who ordered his high spirited and wild cavaliers to charge sword in hand, in three ranks, the pistol to be of secondary importance. Cromwell reduced the ranks to two and eventually trained his men into a steadier body, so disciplined as to be able to rally and re-form after a charge instead of wildly galloping in pursuit over the countryside, as was too often the case with Rupert's cavalry.

To Rupert, however, must be given the credit of the efficient way his patrols carried out their work "of scouring the ways in advance of the army." His vedettes worked in pairs, or in half sections as it was termed in the Great War. These tactics were much in advance of those still in vogue on the Continent, where mounted men were still formed into compact masses of three or more ranks in depth. These, after firing from the saddle often at a totally ineffectual range, would wheel to either flank to envelope their enemy, or to the rear, rank by rank, to reload. These were in fact more or less the tactics initiated by the Schwartz Reiters of unenviable reputation, called Black it is variously stated from the colour of their armour or from their barbaric practice of blackening their faces, which was quite in keeping with their known brutality, but bearing more resemblance to banditti than cavalry soldiers. It would appear that these characteristics have been zealously preserved to the present day.

[1] Ref. The Conduct of the Dk. of Marlborough during the Present War. Published 1712.

FIG. 68. Officers and Trooper of Horse, *c.* 1705.

It has often been mentioned that the charges of Marlborough's cavalry were made at the trot. In support of this it has been pointed out that Marlborough's cavalry at Blenheim attacked moving at the same pace as the infantry and guns, but it by no means follows that this pace was not increased when nearing the enemy, which according to eye-witnesses was what actually did happen, otherwise it is difficult to understand how the allied Horse in two or at most three ranks managed to overthrow the heavy masses of the enemy cavalry drawn up in more or less column formation, as they repeatedly did right through the War, nor has any consideration been taken into account of the crowding and bumping incidental to the movement of such large masses of horses, the swinging scabbards and carbines striking against the animals' flanks, together with the general excitement of both riders and their mounts.

It is true that on the Continent the regulations for cavalry training make no mention of any other pace faster than the trot, and where the weight of solid masses was preferred to speed, which formation of itself, prevented any more rapid movement, the practice of firing when halted within pistol or carbine range would not allow much distance for the sudden acceleration of pace. Their mounts also appear to have been of a heavier and slower type of horse.

As has been noted, the English cavalry had already been trained to charge in three, or even two ranks, relying on speed to counterbalance the weight of compact masses of the enemy.

It is impossible to imagine the fiery Rupert advancing at a post-boy trot at the head of his dashing young hot-heads mounted on their well-bred horses.

The evidence of Marlborough's own officers certainly gives the impression

FIG. 69. Marlborough's Trumpeter, 1705.

that a pace faster than the trot had been adopted. The charge at Blenheim is described as "advancing gently till close to the enemy, and then going in at increased speed." What this speed was may be gathered when we are told that at Ramillies the Scots Greys and Royal Irish Dragoons charged the Régiment du Roi and broke in "*a la hussard*, sword in hand" and at a gallop.

The superiority of Marlborough's training and the true cavalry spirit it inspired in his regiments was strikingly proved throughout his campaigns, where his Horse permanently maintained its unassailable moral supremacy.

The action of Elixem or Elixheim 1705 may be quoted as a good instance, and also as an example of the two schools of training. Here the Bavarian

Household troops and Cuirassiers, who it is stated had never known defeat and in consequence considered themselves the crack cavalry of the period, were drawn up in solid array, their Cuirassiers (like the Austrians) still wearing the heavy cuirass and lobster-tailed helmet of Cromwell's day. Marlborough himself leading the allied cavalry, the front line of which was composed of the British regiments (including the Royal Scots Greys and Irish Dragoons) swept forward into the sunken road and out again up the slope the other side "rides the whirlwind and directs the storm." The Bavarians according to the tactics described above opened a spluttering fire from the saddle and before the smoke had blown away Marlborough at the head of "the whirlwind" of British cavalry had crashed into the Household squadrons and Cuirassier regiments and swept them from the field a broken and panic-stricken mob, together with other squadrons including the Cologne Life Guards, which had come up in support. Not even the brave stand made by the Comte de Caraman with his infantry could stay the rout, and a battery of French artillery being abandoned to their fate were ridden down and captured. These guns were of a curious triple barrelled design (Fig. 68), and one may still be seen at the Rotunda, Woolwich. Marlborough himself was attacked by a huge German, who made a wild slash at the Duke, only to fall igno-miniously from his horse and be taken prisoner by His Grace's trumpeter (Fig. 69). Curiously enough Windham's Horse (the Carabineers) which routed the Bavarian Carabineers, and Wood's Horse (3rd Dragoon Guards) now an amalgamated regiment, were both present in this action. Cadogan's Horse (5th Dragoon Guards) overthrew four squadrons of Bavarian Guards and took four standards. The total number of trophies were 9 standards, 10 guns, and the prisoners included 14 Generals, Brigadiers and Colonels, 14 Majors and Captains and about 40 Subalterns, besides casualties amount-into to 1,000. These were the fruits of this little known but brilliant cavalry action, for which no honour was ever granted (Fig. 68).[1]

The cuirasses which had been handed into store in 1689 were re-issued again in 1707, as Marlborough, writing in French on 4th February, 1707, says: "I must inform you that the Queen has decided to give cuirasses to the English cavalry," and again on the 6th July the same year "that our cavalry have received their cuirasses for some time now." These defences consisted

---

[1] The Wars of Marlborough, by Frank Taylor, article in *Cavalry Journal*. "Elixem" by Major Fitz M. Stacke, M.C.

of a breast plate only and appears to have been worn under the coat, which hides the straps which fasten it. The Blenheim tapestries show general officers with front and back plates worn on the outside of the coat (Fig. 70).

FIG. 70. Regiments of Horse, 1707.

Swords were provided by Colonels of regiments, and were not a standardised pattern or always of English manufacture. The guards, so far as one can judge from paintings, tapestries, etc., seem to have been mostly of the simple "knuckle bow" or three-bar type (Fig. 44).

The Royal Scots Dragoons were armed with the Scottish broad swords at one time, and these, no doubt, were basket hilted.

The carbine, or light musket, is sometimes seen carried attached by a swivel and bar to the shoulder belt and at others with the butt resting on the bucket, the muzzle pointing upwards.

DRAGOONS

Dragoons, who made their appearance during the Civil War, again come into existence, a regiment being raised in 1672 to be disbanded in 1674 and two other regiments raised for War service in the same year only existed until 1678.

Dragoons at this time were really mounted infantry, or in the language of the time, "mounted musketeers" and as such were distinct from the cavalry

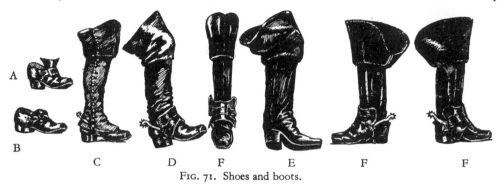

FIG. 71. Shoes and boots.

as is shown by the old terms of "Horse, Foot, and Dragoons." Like the infantry they used a drum, but of a smaller size, so that it could be carried on a man's left side under his bridle arm and even so it must have been cumbersome enough (Fig. 73).

In the Civil War the term Company was used, but this was changed to Troop, as was the rank of Ensign to that of Cornet, in fact already tending towards the transformation into cavalry. As Sir James Turner describes them although they were not strictly cavalry, yet from the fact that they acted with them "they were part of the Horse and subordinate to the General, Lt. General or Major General of Horse and not to those of Foot."

Their horses were smaller and bought at a cheaper rate than those of the cavalry and were used only as a means of rapid movement, being linked together when the time for dismounted action arrived. It is stated that they originally rode in ranks of eleven and the outside man of each rank remained mounted as horse-holder. Sir James Turner says "of ten Dragoons nine fought on foot and the tenth remained with the horses." Their equipment in 1672 was as follows: Twelve men besides the N.C.O.'s were given halberds and a pair of pistols, the remainder being armed with matchlocks, bayonets and swords carried in waistbelts.

FIG. 72. Dragoons, 1672.

Taking the Royal Dragoons as an example, a regiment would have been composed of six troops, each consisting of a Quartermaster, two Sergeants, three Corporals, two Hautboys, two Drummers and fifty private men besides officers. Hautboys are not mentioned on the strength of those regiments raised in 1672.

In 1687 snaphance muskets strapt, with bright barrels 3 feet 8 inches long, buckets, cartouche boxes, bayonets, grenado pouches and hammer hatches were issued.

Strapt muskets would mean muskets fitted with slings and buckets, the leather socket arrangement attached to the front of the saddle to support the weight of the firearm. According to the military text-books of the time the orders to dismount and mount were executed by much the same drill movements as at the present time.

About 1697 pistols ceased to be issued to Dragoon regiments, and between 1695 and 1697 the grenado pouch no longer formed part of their equipment.

Dragoons were dressed in red coats, cloth waistcoats and breeches, but in 1697 the Royal Dragoons wore crimson coats like the cavalry. The officers wore gorgets of the different coloured metals denoting rank in exactly the same way as those of the infantry. Besides the usual laced hat the Dragoon wore a cap; this consisted of a band of fur with a cloth bag similar to that worn by the Grenadiers. In the painting at Hampton Court depicting the arrival of William III at Brixham, Dragoons are to be seen wearing red coats and brown fur caps with red bags or hoods as they were called. The cap corresponds with that shown in other paintings of the period as well as that in pictures of French Dragoons of about this time (Fig. 73).

FIG. 73. Dragoons, 1697.

How long this cap remained in use is uncertain, but it still appears in Dutch prints of the Marlborough campaigns as well as in the Blenheim tapestries (Fig. 74). There has been much speculation as to the type of boot worn by Dragoons; that it differed in some way from that worn by the "Horse" is evident from the fact that it cost considerably less. This was possibly due to its being made of lighter leather than the stiff cavalry boot, (Fig. 71), which seems logical in view of the fact that the Dragoon had to fight on foot (Fig. 71, D), for which service the rigid jack boot would have been singularly unsuitable. The French dragoon wore a leather legging shaped like a boot, laced or buckled down the sides and having a stiff top. These are represented in the Blenheim tapestries but only as being worn by Marlborough and his General Officers. Otherwise there seems to be no difference in the boots worn by the Horse and Dragoons.

Dragoons seem to have been the handy men of the army as besides their training as mounted infantry, which included firing from the saddle and "being strong bold horsemen," their use is recommended in the text-books of the time "for swift marches, passing deep ways or waters, to keep equal pace with the 'Horse' till the Foot at more leisure could come up." They formed the escorts to convoys, etc., and the storming parties during a siege. "They were not to be encamped in the main body of the army but have their camp a little separate at the head or wings to which the greatest danger seems to threaten, as being the out guard of the army." In addition to these duties they appear to have done a certain amount of pioneer work, such as clearing away obstacles in advance of the main body, which, no doubt, was the reason for their being equipped with hatchets. They are also mentioned as making fascines. These they often carried forward mounted and threw into the fosse or trench to enable the infantry to pass over. A regiment, probably intended for the North British Dragoons by their light coloured horses, is shown in the tapestry of the battle of Donauwert, or Schellenberg, carrying fascines across the front of their saddles (Fig. 74). It was in this action that Marlborough used his Dragoons in the rôle of cavalry proper, for having been dismounted in support of the infantry attacks, they were ordered to remount and join the Horse in the final charge which swept the retreating Bavarians into the Danube.

The Royal Dragoons, who had had a previous existence as the Regiment of Tangier Horse, are described by Nathan Brooks at the Review at Putney Heath, October, 1684, commanded by John Lord Churchill "as coated and cloaked red lined blue, their housings embroidered blue and yellow upon red (this sounds as if it might mean a scroll pattern border) with the Royal cypher; Holster caps the same." A clothing estimate of 1699 gives the following details for a Private. "A crimson coat, blue waistcoat and breeches. Pair of blue worsted stockings, a hat with gold orris lace, hat-band of same, carbine belt, waist-belt and cartouche box, sword, bayonet, a good pair of boots with large spurs and spur leathers. Bridle crupper breastplate and collar, holsters tipped brass, bucket, embroidered housings and holster caps, a pair of gloves."

"A Corporal to have broad orris lace about the cuffs." "A Sergeant broad orris gold lace for sleeves and narrow gold orris lace on the cuffs and flaps of coat, narrow orris lace for the belt. Plush carbine belt, waistbelt and cartouche box."

The letters of several officers of this regiment while serving with Stanhope in Spain 1706 to 1712, give many details of uniform and how deficiencies were made up, and tell how regimental distinctions of dress were already cherished. This correspondence, with that of the Scots Greys, was published by the Rev. Percy Sumner in the *Journal of the Society for Army Historical Research.*

FIG. 74. Dragoons, *c.* 1706.

The Colonel is to get General Stanhope "to give as much of the cloathing as was Guiscarts, as will make up what we want and because of the difference of the facings; if you can get any blue, we must try and make up the expense for the facing of the clothes that we must keep to our blue."

Further on we read that a certain number of coats, waistcoats and breeches were found, all of which were taken with 12 blue coats for the hautboys and drummers. The remainder required was made up with coats sent from England, and the officer goes on to state "which were very ill made and of cloth but indifferent. I have had them altered; they are faced with blue, with a slashed sleeve and a cape (collar) which sets them off very much."

CAVALRY

The Colonel's kit includes "Housings and holster caps of scarlet cloth with gold lace and fringe, a scarlet surtout and breeches with silver lace."

The same complaint, which was to be made just a hundred years later in Spain, repeatedly occurs as regards the swords sent from England "as being good for nothing." "There is no dealing with the French but with good swords, they having excellent ones, we are all resolved if we come to Barcelona and we can find German blades to buy them."

In 1709 the officers decided for the next campaign "to make each of them a plain red coat and breeches lined with canvas, a canvas waistcoat embroidered with gold, a red housing and holster caps laced gold with crown and cypher embroidered and each a grey feather (for the hat)." The next winter frocks were made for all the men "by which means they have not worn any of their coats this winter, so that we shall make them serve for the next campaign without turning."

Two independent companies of Dragoons were raised in Scotland 21st May, 1678. They were dressed in grey coats, breeches, helmets or bonnets, and armed with broadswords, bayonets, short muskets with buckets. Further companies were raised, and on 25th November, 1681, they were formed into a regiment and called the Royal (Scots) Dragoons. In 1683 they were still clothed in stone grey cloth coats and again in 1684, although permission was granted to import red or scarlet cloth from England. By 1687 they were dressed in red coats with blue facings and tin buttons. Like other Dragoon regiments they wore caps as well as hats, and in 1688 the regiment entered England. In 1690 Sergeants' loops are mentioned, so we can suppose that they wore coats with laced buttonholes. In 1690–2 loops for officers and Sergeants' coats are mentioned, and in 1692 brass buttons replaced those of tin.

The famous grey horses are mentioned in 1693 in an officer's letter asking for a grey horse to be bought for him.

In the following year we read in Narcissus Luttrell's *Brief Relation of State Affairs:*

"19th April 1694. This day the King took a view of Colonel Cunningham's and Sir Thomas Levington's [Livingston's] Dragoons (Scots Greys) in Hyde Park being two regiments lately come from Scotland. They made a fine show, especially the latter, who were all mounted on grey and white horses, and new clothed and are more like Troopers (of Horse) than Dragoons."

The Royal Regiment of Scots Dragoons, the official title at that time, seem to have been "kittle cattle" to tackle as Evelyn writes "22 April, 1694. Some regiments of Highland (sic) Dragoons were on their march through England; they were of large stature, well appointed and disciplined. One of them having reproached a Dutchman for cowardice in our late fight, was attacked by two Dutchmen, when with his sword he struck off the head of one and cleft the skull of the other down to his chin."

In 1704 the officers of this regiment wore blue breeches and blue waist-coats embroidered with gold, the Subalterns laced belts and the Quarter-masters plain red coats, but the hats of all were to be laced. In 1705 "buff shoulder belts were ordered besides new Grenadier caps to be made to the number of the Grenadiers." This seems to point to these caps being worn by a Grenadier Troop and not by the whole regiment, as hats and cockades are also mentioned in the same list.

White linen frocks lined blue figure in the clothing lists for 1706.

It is often stated that the Royal Irish Dragoons were granted Grenadier caps by Queen Anne as a distinction and this fact is mentioned in the correspondence of different Colonels with the Adjutant General in 1760–68 as the reason for retaining them.

These, however, were not the only Dragoon regiments who had Grenadier Troops; Berkeley's Regiment (4th Hussars) having one in 1690 and in 1708 instructions for clothing, issued by the Board of General Officers, state that "new Greanadier accoutrements, viz: caps and belts as long as the Grenadiers shall be continued."

It was in the Scots Greys that Mrs. Christian Davies, the female dragoon, served until wounded at Ramillies. Her romantic story is briefly as follows: Her husband Richard Welsh having been inveigled by a recruiting officer into enlisting was sent with the drafts to Flanders. Kit Welsh with the view of finding him herself enlisted in a Foot Regiment and served with William III's army in Flanders. Here she fought a duel with a Sergeant whom she seriously wounded, being discharged in consequence. She re-enlisted in the Scots Greys, was wounded at Donauwert, but still managed to conceal her sex and took part in the battle of Blenheim. After this she at last met her husband with another woman, but still continued to serve with the Scots Greys, her husband promising to keep her secret, until at Ramillies, having had her skull fractured by a shell she was carried to hospital where her sex was discovered. A reconciliation with her husband having been effected their marriage was recelebrated, all the officers of the regiment attending, each giving her "a piece of gold, some four or five." After this she still followed the army in the capacity of a sutleress to the end of the campaign. Returning to England she was granted a shilling a day by Queen Anne and ended her days as an Out-Pensioner at Chelsea Hospital and died 7th July, 1739, being buried with military honours, "according to her Desire amongst the old Pensioners in Chelsea Burying Ground." Three volleys were fired over her grave.

The Inniskilling Dragoons are stated to have worn iron grey coats. It is possible that a temporary kit of this colour may have been used when the regiment was first raised, but in any case in 1689 red coats and cloaks were already being sent over to Ireland for them.

In 1692 the Captains had beaver hats, crimson coats lined crimson shalloon with gold lace loops and buttons, ash coloured waistcoats laced with gold and gold fringed belts, embroidered cloth housings and holster caps laced with gold galloon. The Lieutenants, Cornets and Quartermasters had the same uniform and horse furniture but with silver lace instead of gold. "Two embroidered standards." "For the Sergeants, Corporals, Drummers and Hautboys and Private soldiers 462 coats and breeches with like number of housings and holster caps, cartouche boxes, slings for muskets, belts, bayonets gloves, boots, spurs."

In addition there are certain quantities of blue and yellow cloth and blue baize, with silk livery lace and buttons. This, the Rev. Percy Sumner suggests, was for the livery of the Officers' servants, but it seems as if it might just as well be for the Drummers' or Hautboys' uniforms.

TRUMPETERS AND KETTLE DRUMMERS
CAVALRY AND DRAGOONS

The Kettle drummers and Trumpets of Horse and the hautbois, or "hautboys," and drummers of Dragoons are said to have worn coats of their regiments' facing colours.

The small figures of the Trumpeters of the Tangier Horse in the picture of the review at Tangier 1683–4 previously referred to, are shown dressed in red coats with a white or cream sleeveless over-jacket, or buff coat, wide brimmed hats, buff shoulder belts and sashes or waist belts. Their trumpets are silver; they are mounted on black, brown or white horses. The Kettle-drummer wears the same dress and rides a black horse, his kettle-drum banners are red and embroidered with some device.

The Great Wardrobe accounts from 1678 onwards contain a mass of information concerning the Royal livery worn by the Life Guards and their troops of Horse Grenadiers, together with certain other regiments who enjoyed the same privilege. From the various details scattered here and there in the different bills, Warrants, etc., the Royal livery seems in most cases to have born a close resemblance to that of the State dress worn to-day by the Trumpeters and Band of the Household Cavalry.

Beginning with the Kettle Drummers and Trumpeters of the Troops of Life Guards, during the years 1678–1689, these were crimson velvet coats with blue velvet cuffs and blue serge linings, laced all over with gold and silver lace and gold and silver buttons. This lacing included silver and gold buttonhole loops, blue breeches, red cloth cloaks lined blue and laced down before with gold and silver. Hats laced gold and silver with hatbands of the same, black velvet caps, white leather belts stitched with silver and having gilt buckles.

In 1690 the coats for the 1st, 2nd and 3rd Troops were crimson with blue velvet cuffs and trimmed with broad and narrow gold and silver orris lace with a gold twist between. Their Majesties' cypher and crown embroidered on the front and back. The cloak was crimson with blue velvet cape laced with gold and silver and looped with gold and silver down the front. These cloaks were also furnished with neck loops. Breeches of blue velvet, belt laced gold and silver, hat laced gold and silver. The Kettle Drum banners were embroidered with their Majesties' arms and supporters, fringed with gold and silver and tied with blue ribbon. The Trumpet banners were similar but smaller and furnished with gold and silver strings and tassels.

In 1696, April 16th. For the 1st, 2nd and 3rd Troops the same description except the coat was laced with broad gold orris with a gold orris twist between, buff belt laced gold, hatband and hat laced gold, crimson breeches; the Trumpet banner tassels and strings now being crimson, blue, gold and buff.

CAVALRY

April 25th the same year, another bill gives the coats laced with silk and silver as usual.

During Queen Anne's reign the uniform was much the same. The 1706 entry is for "coats of crimson velvet all trimmed with broad gold orris lace and gold twist between, embroidered back and front with H.M.'s letters A. R., crowns and knots between the letters, crimson breeches: crimson cloak lined blue and trimmed with broad orris lace down before and round the capes and cuffs of blue

FIG. 75. Trumpeters of the Life Guards, c. 1689.

velvet; buff belts laced gold orris and gilt buckles. Hats laced gold with gold hat bands and a gold button. Black velvet caps. The Kettle Drum Banners with H.M.'s arms and supporters scrolls and motto, '*Semper eadem*,' gold fringes and tied with blue ribbons. Trumpet strings with large tassels of gold, crimson, blue and buff silk."

The silver lace seems now to have disappeared.

The velvet (jockey) caps and the gold twist are interesting, as being still in existence, the gold twist being the gold chain pattern between the broad gold lace on the State clothing. The crimson cloaks with gold laced blue collar are still the same.

Hautbois and Drummers of the Troops of Horse Grenadiers:

1678 Red cloaks, blue breeches and stockings.

1688 1st Troop Horse Grenadiers, red cloth coats faced blue with 60 loops and 48 buttons per coat, blue breeches, belts and hats laced with silver.

1689 2nd Troop, crimson cloth coats faced blue, trimmed with silk and silver lace and black velvet, their Majesties' cypher and crown embroidered on the back, blue breeches, hats laced gold and silver, black velvet caps, belts stitched silver, red cloth cloak faced blue serge.

1689 For 1st, 2nd and 3rd Troops, gold and silver open lace chain work for hats, coats with 4½ dozen blue, gold and silver-plated and tufted loops.

1689 For 12 Hautbois and 6 Drums of 1st, 2nd and 3rd Troops, 432 yds. broad crimson blue gold colour white and silver lace, 180 yds. ditto buttonhole lace, 792 yds. black velvet lace.

1690 Purple leather belts embroidered with silver.

1691 For 1st, 2nd and 3rd Troops as before, but with crimson coats trimmed narrow gold orris, hats and belts laced with gold.

1692 2nd Troop crimson coat with broad silk and silver lace and a black velvet lace, cypher and crown embroidered on the backs. Hats lace and band gold and silver, velvet caps.

1696 The same.

1702–1706 Crimson coats lined and faced blue, trimmed with broad and narrow gold lace, crimson breeches, leather belt stitched with gold, gold laced hat and band, black velvet cap, crimson cloak faced blue and laced round the (blue) cape with narrow gold orris.

1711 The same, but a purple leather belt.

Before going further it will be advisable to glance at the pictorial evidence,

The first representation is of the Kettle Drummer and Trumpeters in the Coronation procession of Charles II. These no doubt are wearing scarlet jackets laced with gold and silver, but as no description exists it is worthless to conjecture. Their chief interest beyond showing the type and cut of the dress is their Drum and Trumpet banners, which are embroidered with the Royal Arms and supporters, have deep lace fringes. In the book of standards and colours captured by the armies of Louis XIV is a sketch of the Kettle Drum banner of the Life Guards (Fig. 76) taken at Landen or Neerwinden 1693, where, with five other regiments of horse, the Life Guards repeatedly charged the overwhelming masses of French cavalry in order to cover the retreat of the infantry.

In the series of engravings of the funeral procession of George Monk, Duke of Albemarle, is a trumpeter dressed in a coat with hanging sleeves and hat ornamented with a band and knot of ribbons. His heavily fringed trumpet banner is embroidered with the Royal Arms and supporters. This

CAVALRY

man may possibly be a trumpeter of the Duke's Troop of Life Guards, as these wore ribbons in their hats instead of feathers.

After this there is the Scots Troop of Life Guards (Fig. 61). These, from the rather indistinct details, appear to have their coats ornamented down the front with bands of broad lace; the cuffs, pocket flaps and waist-coats are also edged with lace and possibly down the seams.

FIG. 76.
Drum Banner of the Life Guards, 1693.

In another engraving of this series is a group of trumpeters with coats laced down the seams and skirts and having bands of lace round the sleeves and on their sword belts. The hanging sleeves are clearly indicated in these engravings. The hanging sleeves, it should be noticed in these cases, are more in the form of hanging bands of laced cloth attached to the shoulder and to the waist.

FIG. 77.
Trumpeters of the Life Guards, c. 1689.

The engravings of State cere-monies in the reign of William and Mary show various figures of Trumpeters and here the lace buttonhole loops down the front and on the pocket flaps are a distinct feature; in some places the dark tufts at the end of the loops are clearly shown. Both caps and hats are shown, the former with the peak turned up or down, and in one instance the cap is ornamented with a long hanging plume (Figs. 75 and 77).

In the background of a portrait of General Schomberg are a Kettle Drummer and Trumpeters (Fig. 78). They are dressed in scarlet coats laced down the seams with gold and embroidered back and front with the Royal

FIG. 78. Negro Kettle Drummer and Trumpeter, *c.* 1690.

cypher and crown. The sleeves are close fitting at the wrist and have no cuffs
or turn-up of facing colour. The coat linings are a deep buff colour. The
Trumpeters' hats are laced with gold and ornamented with white feathers.
The Kettle Drummer is a negro in a similar uniform and wears a small white
turban bound round a blue cloth cap with a hanging hood or bag. The
Drum and Trumpet banners are red embroidered and fringed with gold.
The housings appear to be the same.

It may be mentioned that in the early part of the seventeenth century the
Trumpeter held a position of considerable importance and was counted as
a non-combatant. In evidence of this he carried a sword with a broken point.
He was chosen, besides his musical talent, for his diplomatic gifts and tact,
as it was he who was sent as parlementair to arrange a truce or the conditions
of surrender, and as such was always held immune from capture. This was
probably the origin of sending a Trumpeter to accompany the white
flag.

CAVALRY

The Kettle Drummer, unlike the Trumpeter, was not considered a non-combatant, but "should be a man of courage preferring to perish in the fight than allow himself and his drums to be captured." The drums and their banners were held in as much esteem as a regiment's colours, and were always mentioned in the list of trophies captured from an enemy together with the colours, standards and guns.

To return to the Wardrobe accounts. The next regiment mentioned is the (Earl of Oxford's) Regiment of Horse. The description of the livery of the Kettle Drummer and Trumpeters in 1689 corresponds exactly in every detail with that of the Life Guards down to the crimson coats looped and laced with gold and silver with gold drawn lace between, the laced hat and velvet cap and blue breeches. The Drum and Trumpet banners are embroidered with the Royal Arms and supporters and fringed gold and silver. In 1699 the various changes are also the same, i.e. crimson breeches and gold lace; Drum and Trumpet banners with gold, crimson, blue and buff tassels and strings.

The same details of badges, lace, etc., are given during Queen Anne's reign, so that it is unnecessary to repeat them.

The Queen's Horse. This regiment's Kettle Drummer and Trumpeters also had the privilege of wearing the Royal livery as the entry for 1678 states: "16 Trumpet and Kettle Drum banners of crimson with gold and silver fringes, strings and tassels, with our Royal Arms embroidered on both sides as those of our said dearest consorts Troops of Guards are."

1692. Crimson cloth coats faced blue velvet and laced with gold and embroidered on the back and front with their Majesties' crown and cypher. The Drum and Trumpet banners of crimson damask embroidered with the crown and cypher and fringed with silver with crimson and silver tassels and strings.

There is no mention of silver lace for the coats and cloaks or of velvet caps. The cloaks are of crimson cloth laid down before and on the capes with the said velvet (blue) and gold lace and faced or lined with red serge. In one of the mural paintings at Marlborough House a group of Trumpeters and a Kettle Drummer are depicted in the background and consequently not very distinct as regards details. They are all wearing coats of yellowish buff cloth with hanging sleeves. The Trumpet banners match the coats, apparently a case of the Trumpeters wearing coats of the facing colour (Fig. 79). They

FIG. 79. Kettle Drummer and Trumpeters, 1709.

may be intended to represent Cadogan's Horse (5th D.G.s) who had previously buff facings, although by 1711 these are described as green. Lumley's (1st D.G.s) had yellow facings, but their Trumpeters wore the Royal livery.

The Royal Dragoons while in Spain in 1708 at least dressed their hautbois in blue coats.

The Queen's Dragoons (3rd King's Own Hussars) in 1713 wore the Queen's Royal livery and blue feathers in their hats.

High personages and Generals on State missions or in command of armies also had Kettle Drummers and Trumpeters attached to their personal staff. These wore the Royal livery of crimson faced with blue velvet, laced and looped with gold and silver and gold laced hats, the details of which agree closely with those of the same dates already described.

In 1672 a Kettle Drummer and four Trumpeters were to attend the Marquess of Blanquefort beyond the seas. In this instance mention is made of "silver fringed scarfs "such as have been formerly delivered to H.M.'s Trumpeters.

1687. "A Kettle Drummer and 6 Trumpeters for Ireland to attend Lord Tyrconnel."

1702, 1705, 1708. Two Trumpeters to attend the Duke of Marlborough. Here the crimson livery coat and cloak together with hats and waist belts are laced with gold; the breeches of crimson cloth; the Trumpet banners with the Royal Arms, supporters, scroll and motto exactly like those of the Life Guards. The velvet caps are also included in the list.

APPENDIX

REFERENCES TO CAVALRY, 1660–1714

Life Guards.

1684. King's Troop. Scarlet coats lined blue, velvet carbine belts laced gold and silver. Red housings and holster caps embroidered with Royal cypher and crown.

Horse Grenadiers. Red coats lined blue with blue loops tufted with yellow. Grenadier caps lined blue with a blue roundel at the back.

Queen's Troop. As above, but with green facings, housings and holster caps. Green velvet carbine belts laced gold.

Horse Grenadiers. Green loops with yellow tufts.

The Duke's Troop. Same as above, but with yellow facings, etc. Carbine belts laced silver.

Horse Grenadiers. Yellow loops.

[Nathan Brooks. Review at Putney Heath, 1684.]

SANDFORD'S HISTORY OF THE CORONATION OF JAMES II

1st Troop. The officers richly habited either in coats of crimson velvet embroidered with gold and silver or fine scarlet cloth embroidered or laced with gold and silver or both intermixed. They wore scarfs about their waists of gold or silver network, or crimson taffeta richly fringed with gold or silver on the edges and with a deep fringe of the same at the ends. Their cloaks were also of fine scarlet cloth embroidered on the capes and down before with gold or silver or both intermixed. In their hats they wore tours of white feathers. Their houses and holster caps being crimson richly embroidered with gold and silver and the manes cruppers and tayls of their horses were garnished with large knots of broad blue taffeta ribbands.

The gentlemen of this Troop (200 in number) were all new

clothed in coats and cloaks of scarlet cloth lined blue chalon, the facings of their sleeves of the same stuff were laced about with a figured galoon of silver edged with gold two inches broad. Their buttons were of silver plate. They each of them had a good buff coat and a large pair of gauntlet gloves of the same. In their hats (which were black and turned up on one side and edged about with a broad silver lace), they wore large blue knots of broad taffata ribband which blew, being the distinguishing colour of their Troop from the others, the heads of their horses were adorned with knots of like ribbands.

They were extraordinarily well mounted and excellently equipped, having their houses and holster caps of scarlet cloth imbroidered with the King's cypher and crown within a border of foliage. Each of these gentlemen was armed and accoutred with a good broad sword and large buff shoulder belt, a case of pistols, a carbine with a carbine belt of blew velvet 5 inches broad bordered with figured silver galoon (edged with a narrow gold lace) in breadth 2 inches, so that not above an inch in breadth of velvet appeared.

1st Troop of H.M. Horse Grenadiers. The officers of this troop of Horse Grenadiers were richly habited and equiped agreable in colour to the 1st Troop of Horse Guards, being very well mounted and accoutred. The Lieutenants lead the Troop when it marched on foot, with half Pikes, the sergeants armed with partisans and the corporals with halberts.

The Grenadiers 60 in number were clothed in coats of fine red cloth lined and faced with blue chalon and buttoned with white metal hatched with silver on the breast arms and faceings of the sleeves they wore large loops of fine blue worsted edgeded and tufted with black and white. The crowns of their caps were raised to a high point falling back at the top in form of a capouch, which were turned up before and behind triangular and faced with blue plush and on the back of the crowns was a roundel or grenado ball also of the same.

Their cloaks were of fine cloth lined with blew, their hats being black and laced about with silver were buttoned up and adorned with knots of blew taffata ribband, as were the heads of their horses. Their holster caps and houses (scallapt on the edges) of red cloth were embroidered with the Royal cypher and crown and bordered with foliage, so that being annexed or depending on H.M. 1st Troop of Horse Guards this troop was agreable to them in all their colours. Each of these Grenadiers was armed and accoutred with a long carbine strapped, a good sword with waist buff belt, a case of pistols, cartouch box, bucket, bionet, and Grenado Pouch.

2nd Troop. H.M. Horse Grenadiers. The officers of the 2nd Troop were richly habited, and suitable, in the colour of their housings and holster caps (which were of green velvet, and in their ribbands of green Taffaty) to the officers of the 2nd Troop of Horse Guards, being also excellently mounted and equipped.

The Grenadiers also (60 in number) were cloathed, armed and accoutred in all respects answerable to the first Troop of Horse Grenadiers, but were differing from them in the colour of their houses, holster caps, linings, facings and worsted loops (edged and tufted black and white), which were all green (the distinguishing colour of the 2nd Troop of Horse Guards) and their caps faced with green plush. They wore gilt buttons and their hats edged about with gold lace, were adorned with large knots of green Taffaty ribband, their horses' heads being garnished with the same.

3rd Troop. The officers of this troop of Guards were richly habited and excellently well mounted and equipped in like manner as were those of the 1st Troop from whom they differed only in the colour of their houses and holster caps which were yellow velvet, and in the garnishing of the manes, cruppers and tayles of their horses being with yellow ribbands. The gentlemen of this troop (200) were clothed and accoutred in like manner as the 1st and 2nd Troops, but differing both in the lace of their hats of their sleeves, facings and their carbine belts, which was of silver and in the colours of the ribbands in their hats and horses' heads, which were yellow, as was also the cloth of the houses and holster caps and the velvet facings of their carbine belts.

3rd Troop. Horse Grenadiers. The officers are richly habited and suitable in the colour of their houses and holster caps to the officers of the 3rd Troop of Horse Guards, being yellow velvet and their ribbands of the same colour.

Queen's Regiment of Horse (1 DGs.).

1686. Red coats lined yellow.

1687. Stolen property of a Quarter Master, red coat lined yellow silk with large plate buttons. Sleeves faced with silver tissue, a silver net scarf, silver fringed gloves, white holland waistcoat with silver fringe, black hat laced and silver hat band, a periwig.

1692. Trumpeters and Kettle Drummers crimson cloth coat lined blue and faced with blue velvet, gold orris lace and gold thread buttons, embroidered back and front with their Majesties' crown and cypher. Cloaks of red cloth laced down before and on the capes with said velvet and gold lace and faced red serge.

(*2nd DGs.*)

1686. Red lined red.

1694. Red lined buff (*London Gazette*).

(*3rd DGs.*)

1686. Red lined green.

1692. Crimson coats lined green, grey waistcoats. Red cloaks faced green. Horses all colours.

[Treasury State Papers.]

Arran's Horse (4th DGs.).

1686. Red lined white and white sashes.

1700. Red lined white, white waistcoats and pewter buttons, red clack lined red. (*London Gazette*).

(*5th DGs.*)

1686. Red lined buff.

1689. Red lined white. (*London Gazette*).

1692. A deserter, brown wig, red coat lined white, pewter buttons, striped stuff waistcoat, and red shag breeches striped. Another deserter, flaxen hair, grey coat (i.e. undress), striped stuff waistcoat, hat edged silver.

1700. Red lined white, white waistcoats, cloaks red lined red, pewter buttons.

1711. Cadogan's Horse. A deserter, brown wig with black bag (i.e. hair bag), silver laced hat, red coat faced green with broad silver lace on the sleeves, green waistcoat, green shag breeches. Trooper's saddle and green horse cloth under it. (*London Gazette*.)

(6th DGs.).

1686. Red lined green.

1688. Deserter "took away with him new blue velvet saddle with silver twist, holster caps the same."

1st or Royal Dragoons.

1684. Coated and cloaked red lined blue, housings embroidered with blue and yellow upon red, with the Royal cypher, holster caps the same, with the Royal cypher. (Nathan Brooks, Review on Putney Heath.)

1699. Oct. 2nd. Privates crimson coat, blue waistcoat and breeches, blue stockings, gold laced hat with gold hat band, carbine belt, waist belt and cartouch box, sword and bayonet, boots, spurs and spur leathers. Bridle and crupper, breastplate and collar, holsters tipped brass; bucket, housings and holster caps embroidered, pair of gloves.

A Corporal to have broad orris lace on the cuffs.

A Sergeant, a broad and narrow gold lace to the sleeves and broad lace on pocket flaps, narrow gold lace for the belt; plush carbine belt, waist belt and cartouch box. (Thomas Hall, Clothier, Estimate.)

1700. Deserters, crimson lined blue, hats with broad gold lace.

(3rd Dragoons).

"Waist-coats and breeches blue." (Treasury State Papers, c. 1692.)

Captain Hamilton's Troop of Dragoons in Ireland.

1684. July 31st. 60 sets of brass plates for fusees, etc. Two coats as patterns. For officers, blue coat laced and lined red. Plain red coat lined white, with worsted loops for privates. 1 blue cloak lined red; velvet embroidered saddlery for officers; 2 belts,

1 with gold galoon, 1 stitched, 2 dragoon caps, 1 of blue velve
lined fur, 1 of blue cloth lined red.

> (Ref. Out letters Customs, IX, pp. 21–2. *Calendar
> Treasury Book.*)

1st Regiment of Horse of Inniskilling.
> 1689. Red cloaks faced red; red coats lined red; hats, red breeches,
> shoulder belts, cartouch boxes, holster caps and housings, boots,
> gloves, 6 standards and belts. For officers blue coats . . . hats.

2nd Regiment of Horse of Inniskilling.
> 1689. Red cloaks faced with green, red coats lined green. The rest as
> for 1st Regiment.
> > (Ref. Cloathing sent to Ireland.)

Two Troops of Dragoons of Inniskilling.
> 1689. Red coats faced   ; red cloaks; 110 waist belts; 4 shoulder
> belts.

Macclesfield's Horse.
Red coats lined grey. Grey cloaks. (*London Gazette*, April 1695.)
Galway's Horse.
> 1688. Light grey coats lined red, brass buttons, black hats laced galoon,
> buff shoulder belts, swords, carbines and pistols.

FIG. 80. Standard and Pouch of Killigrew's (8th) Dragoons. 1707.

COLOURS

As this subject has been most exhaustively treated by S. M. Milne in his standard work, *Standards and Colours of the Army*, and what is written here is very largely quoted from his book, it may be asked why we have included it in the present volume. The answer is that only 200 copies of Milne's book were printed and is therefore not now easily obtainable, and also that fresh sources of information have since come to light which fill in certain gaps.

In 1672 Captain Thomas Venn published a work entitled *Military Observations or Tactics put into Practice for the Exercise of Horse and Foot, the Original Ensigns, the Postures of the Colours . . .*

It is with the part referring to colours that we are here concerned, as he gives certain principles for the design of colours which were adhered to during the reign of Charles II to that of Queen Anne and which are still maintained to a certain extent in the colours of the Brigade of Guards to this day. He writes: "The Colonel's colour should be of a pure clean colour without any mixture, the Lieutenant-Colonel's only with St. George's armes in the upper corner next the staff, the Majors the same but with a little stream blazant and every Captain with St. Georges alone, but with so many spots or several devices as pertain to the dignity of their several places."

Now although the date of publication of Venn's work is 1672, there are several indications that the contents refer to a much earlier period. On looking at the sketches of the sets of colours for 1644 (Fig. 9) we see the principles advocated by Venn already in use as the accepted scheme for the design of infantry colours. When this was started we are unable to say, but there are many examples to be found on the colours of both sides during the Civil War.

The Cavalry being raised by Troops, their cornets bore badges or emblems according to the taste or sentiments of the commanding officer. This custom, however, disappeared when the Troops became regimented and their standards took on some form of uniformity.

It should be noted that both Royalists and Parliamentarians used the Cross of St. George on their ensigns. The Army of the Covenant used the Cross of St. Andrew.

With the Restoration this cross seems to have covered the whole field instead of being placed in the upper canton near the staff as heretofore.

The first notice of regimental colours in Charles II's reign is in a Royal Warrant of February 13th, 1661, requiring "12 colours or ensigns to be made for our Regt. of Foot Guards (Grenadier Guards) of white and red taffeta of the usual largeness with stands heads and tassels, each to have such distinction of some of our Royal badges painted in oil as our trusty and well beloved servant Sir Edward Walker Knight, Garter King of Arms, shall direct."

Another Warrant of March, 1661 for 12 similar colours for the King's Own Regiment of Foot Guards at Dunkirk; the badges are not mentioned, but a water colour drawing belonging to the Grenadier Guards and which is stated to be the design for these ensigns, gives their appearance in full detail. What would be the Royal Standard is plain white with C. R. and crown in gold; the remainder are white with the red cross of St. George having the different company badges placed in the centre.

For the regiment of Irish Foot Guards a Warrant of 1662 gives "yellow and crimson taffeta for 12 colours with our badges painted and guilded thereon." From this it seems possible that these ensigns were yellow with a crimson cross, but what the badges were the Warrant does not say. In the painting of the Review at Tangier beforementioned, the colours, about four in number, are shown grouped in the centre of each regiment. They are mostly of one or two designs, viz., a red Cross of St. George edged white covering the whole flag with yellowish-coloured rays issuing from the four angles of the cross, the whole on either a dark red or very dark colour, probably blue or black. The other type is the red cross throughout on a dark blue or white field. Two regiments which may possibly be intended for the Foot Guards having the first a plain dark red flag, the remaining three red with the St. George's Cross edged white with gold rays from the angles. The other has a set of plain red colours with the cross edged white. The Royal Scots are discernible by their set of blue colours with the white saltire. Still another body of Foot have a curious set closely resembling Union Jacks. It should be remembered that for this Review the seamen from the warships were landed and dressed in the uniform coats of the soldiers, so it is possible that these represent one of those naval detachments which, having no colours, are displaying the "Jacks" from the ships.

COLOURS

Cosmo Duke of Tuscany was present at a Review in Hyde Park in 1669 and noted that the colours of Russell's (1st Foot Guards) were white with a red cross and that the Coldstream had a green colour with six white balls and a red cross. The six white balls seem to indicate the colours of the 6th Captain's company in which case it is possible that the white balls were placed on a red cross. The green colours of the Coldstream were later changed to a set of blue as at a Review on Putney Heath in 1684 they are described as "flying a St. George's Cross bordered white on a blue field."

It is worth while here giving the colours of the various regiments present at the Review.

"1st Regt. of Foot Guards. The Royal Standard carried by the King's Company is crimson throughout with the cypher and crown embroidered in gold"; in fact practically as it has remained ever since, the King's Colour of all Guards' regiments being crimson to this day.

"The Lt.-Colonels the same with C. R., and crown in gold. "The Major C. R. and crown and the stream blazant crimson. 1st Captain's Company a Lion passant guardant crowned or standing on a crown or. 2nd Captain a Rose and Crown, 3rd a Fleur de lys and crown."

"The Colestream, or Cauldstream Regiment of Foot Guards, St. George's Cross bordered white on a blue field."

"The Royal Regiment commanded by the Earl of Dumbarton a St. Andrew's Cross with a thistle and crown circumscribed in the centre 'Nemo me impune lacessit.'"

The Queen's Regiment, Col. Hon. Percy Kirk, "a red cross bordered with white and rays as the Admiral's in a green field. Her Majesty's cypher in the centre."

The Duke of Albany's Maritime Regt. The Admirals: "a red cross with rays of the sun issuing from each angle of the cross or."

The Holland Regt. (The Buffs) "flyes the red cross bordered white on a green field."

Her Royal Highness the Duchess of York and Albany's Regiment: "A red cross (of St. George) bordered white in a yellow field with Rays as that of the Admirals with Her Royal Highnesses cypher in the centre."

In 1676 a composite regiment of Foot was formed of Companies from the various regiments.

The following pairs of Colours were issued to each of the five Companies:

[129]

Captain Sir Herbert Jeffrey's Coy., 2 Colours with crowned Lyon passant upon ye crowne.

Captain Pick's Coy. 2 colours with the Royall Oak crowned.

Captain Mutlowe's, 2 colours, ground blew with a red crosse in a white field.

Captain Middleton's, 2 Colours, the field white waved with lemon mixt with ye red crosse quite throughout with JDY in cypher in gold.

Captain Wm. Meoles, in the Holland regiment under the command of John Earle of Mulgrave, two colours the ground green with a red cross in a white field.

In the Orderly Room of the Grenadier Guards is a set of water colour drawings of the colours and company badges of this regiment. These are said to have been made by Charles II himself. They certainly appear to be a set of designs submitted for approval and have most interesting corrections and alterations made in pencil. The company numbers on the badges have been changed from those originally marked on the drawings and the badges themselves have additions or parts of the design crossed out. If these drawings were not actually made by Charles himself, it certainly looks as if he had made the pencil corrections on them. A point to be noted is that the badges, as corrected, appear on the finished drawings in the Colour book in the Royal Library, Windsor. Besides these badges, two others are shown which do not appear in the Colour Book: one single ostrich feather, possibly the original idea for the two ostrich feathers in saltire of the 23rd Coy. and the white hart issuing from the gate of a castle shown as the 24th Company's badge in the 1751 Colour Book. This Colour Book consists of the designs for the new regimental colours to be issued on the accession of James II, but besides these it gives the colours of the 1st and 2nd Foot Guards of His late Majesty Charles II.

These are described in Sandford's description of the coronation of James II as follows: "In the time of His late Majesty they had been distinguished by Royal badges placed in the centre of each colour. The King's Standard of his own company was of crimson taffeta embroidered with 2 CCs interlaced under the Imperial crown of gold. The Colonels ensign was of white taffeta with a cross of crimson taffeta throughout (as were all the other ensigns) and differenced with an Imperial crown of gold only, the L' Colonels with CR in gold, the Major with a CR and a pile wavy, the

COLOURS

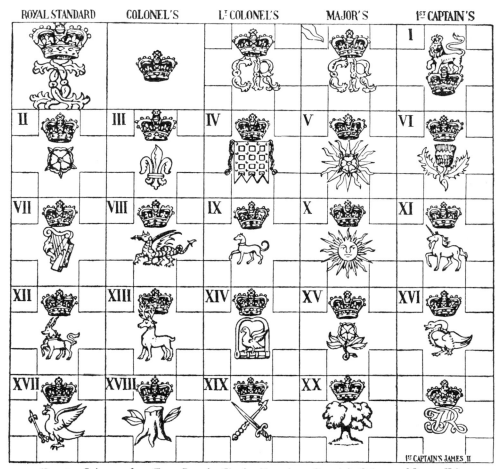

ROYAL STANDARD	COLONEL'S	L.̄ COLONEL'S	MAJOR'S	1.ˢᵗ CAPTAIN'S
				I
II	III	IV	V	VI
VII	VIII	IX	X	XI
XII	XIII	XIV	XV	XVI
XVII	XVIII	XIX	XX	1.ˢᵗ CAPTAIN'S JAMES II

FIG. 81. Colours of 1st Foot Guards, Charles II, and 1st Captain's Colours of James II.[1]

1st Captain with the Kings crest of gold, the II Captain a golden Rose, the III a golden Flowerdelice, the IV with a Portcullis gold, the V a white rose with a sun gold, the VI a thistle gold the stalk and leaves proper, the VII a harp gold, the VIII a gold dragon, the IX a white greyhound with a collar and rings gold, the X a sun of gold, the XI a white unicorn with horn mane and hoofs gold, the XII a white antelope with horns gold acolled with a coronet and chained gold, XII a white hart attired gorged with a coronet chained gold, XIV a white falcon within a fetterlock gold, XV a

---

[1] Only the central portion of the "Colour" is shown, and the Company numbers, for better delineation, are placed near the centre, instead of in the upper corner near the spear head.

[131]

rose and stalk of gold with barbe and leaves of the same, XVI a white swan gorged with a coronet and chained gold, XVIII, a white falcon crowned and grasping a scepter in the pounces of the right foot gold, the XVIII a wood stock erased and trunked gold, XIX a sword and scepter in salter gold, except the blade which is proper, XX the Royal Oak gold, all which badges (except those of the Colonel and eldest Captain) were ensigned with Imperial crowns of gold. The seniority of the captains was distinguished by the numeral letters to XX inclusive painted in black on the dexter canton of the first quarter. The colours of 'the 2nd Regiment of Foot Guards called the Coldstreamers' were blue taffeta, the Colonels plain blue, the L'Colonels blue with crimson cross of St. George edged white as were the ten other ensigns, only the Majors ensign was distinguished by a white pile wavy, issuing out of the canton of the first quarter and the several captains by numeral letters painted in white on the dexter cantons or first quarters. These ensigns were designed by Mr. Francis Sandford for His Grace George late Duke of Albemarle when he commanded this regiment and by his present Majesty when Duke of York" (Fig. 81).

For the coronation James II ordered that the companies of the 1st Regiment of Foot Guards should be distinguished as follows:

"The Standard of His Majesty's company was of crimson taffeta embroidered in the centre with the Royal crown and cypher viz: J R interlaced in gold.

"The Colonels, also of crimson, was not charged with any distinction or device. The Lt.-Colonels was white with the cross of St. George throughout (as were the 21 remaining ensigns) in the middle of which was painted an Imperial crown of gold. The Majors colour was distinguished by the pile wavy of crimson taffeta issuing out of the dexter chief of the first quarter and an Imperial crown of gold in the centre of the colour.

"The eldest Captain had his colours distinguished by one of the King's cyphers and an Imperial crown painted in the middle of the cross; the 2nd Captain two crowns and cyphers; the 3rd Captain three and so on to the 20th Captain, who had his cross charged with 20 cyphers and crowns."

At the same time the following alterations were made in the ensigns of the 2nd Regiment of Foot Guards "that they might be more agreable to the colours of the 1st Regiment," for excepting the Colonel's ensign, which was purely of white taffeta throughout the other eleven were charged with crosses of crimson throughout; the Lt.-Colonel's without distinction;

the Major's a pile wavy. The cross of the eldest Captain was charged in the centre with the numeral letter I in white ensigned with an Imperial crown thereon; the second with II, the third III and so forward to the ninth Captain, who was distinguished by IX each of them under an Imperial crown of gold. Thus did these ensigns fly at the coronation. It will be noticed that there is a difference between the drawings in the Colour book and Sandford's text, in which he says that in the centre of the Lt.-Colonel's and the Major's ensigns is the crown, whereas the red cross is drawn without any device.

With the 2nd or Coldstreamers there is again a variation, Sandford stating the Lt.-Colonel's and Major's were plain, but a crown is shown in the centre of both in the drawings. It seems possible, therefore, that Sandford's description for the two regiments has been reversed.

From the Wardrobe accounts we find that in 1689 the 1st Guards still had crimson and white ensigns, the standard of the King's Company being embroidered and the remainder painted with their Majesties' cypher distinction and crown. Two pairs of crimson and gold tassels and strings and 22 pairs of white and silver are also included. In 1696 ensign staves with gilded spears are mentioned.

The Coldstream also seem to have continued to have the crimson and white ensigns, the standard of the King's Company being embroidered. These colours are also decorated by crowns, cyphers and distinctions; crimson and gold tassels for the Standard and silk tassels and strings for the remainder. In 1696 gold and silver tassels and strings are mentioned for the Standard.

The colours given to the Scots Guards by Charles II in 1650 were ordered to be as follows:

"For the Colonell in a blue field His Majesty's coat or arms viz: Scotland England France and Ireland quartered without any crown over them, and on the other side in great gold letters the words 'Covenant for Religione King and Kingdome,' Lt. Colonel azure a unicorne argent, the other side as the first. Major azure with a lion rampant or, the other side as the first. 1st Captain 3 floure de lices in an azure field 2nd Captain or a lion rampant genelles, in the middle of an azure ensigne 3rd Captain azure, 3 lioncelles gradient or. 4th Captain azure, a harp or, fringed argent. All four ensignes were to have the same words on the other side as on Colonels."

The colours issued in 1662 are described as *Red* with a saltire of St.

Andrew's Cross argent on a blue field and a thistle crowned with this motto round the thistle "Nemo me impune lacessit."

The History of the Scots Guards states that in 1664 His Majesty's coat-of-arms displaced the crowned thistle.

The MS. Colour Book at Windsor has drawings of four colours for the Scots Guards, the Colonel's plain white, Lt.-Colonel's a white Cross of St. Andrew on a blue field, Major's the same with the red pile wavy on the white arm of the cross issuing from the corner near the pike head. 1st Captain's as the Colonel's, but with the numeral I on the blue above the cross.

The Royal Regiment of Foot (Earl of Dumbarton) Colonel's plain white in the centre a thistle, crown over with the motto "Nemo me impune lacessit." Lt.-Colonel's blue with the St. Andrew's Cross, the same device in the centre of the cross as the Colonel's; Major's the same with a red pile wavy; 1st Captain's as the Lt.-Colonel's with the numeral I in silver.

The Queen Dowager's Regiment (2nd or Queen's Regiment). Colonel's plain sea green with the cypher of Queen Catherine of Braganza, two C's interlaced in gold with crown over; Lt.-Colonel's sea green with St. George's Cross bordered white with fine gold rays issuing from the corners, cypher and crown in centre; Major's the same with a white pile wavy; 1st Captain's as the Lt.-Colonel's with a gold numeral I over the crown.

The Holland Regiment (later the Buffs). Colonel's black with a "sun in splendour"; Lt.-Colonel's black with St. George's Cross bordered white with the sun as before; Major's the same with a pile wavy in silver; 1st Captain's as Lt.-Colonel's, with the numeral I in the upper canton.

The Queen's Majesty's Regiment (4th Foot). Colonel's plain white with the Queen's cypher MEBR in gold with a crown above (Marie Eleanore Beatrice Regina). Lt.-Colonel's white with St. George's Cross and in each quarter five eagles sable, beaked and legged or; Major's the same with a red pile wavy; 1st Captain's as Lt.-Colonel's, but with Queen's cypher and crown in the centre of the cross.

The Royal Regiment of Fusiliers (Earl of Dartmouth). The MS. states "the regiment had but three colours of such kind of trophee." The book shows four, however, Colonel's white with trophy of standards, cannon, etc., in gold, in the centre an elaborate escutcheon with stag's head (an armorial bearing of the Earl of Dartmouth Master General of the Ordnance). Lt.-Colonel's white with a St. George's Cross with trophies in the four angles

FIG. 82. Colours of Foot Regiments, 1685–1686.

of the cross; Major's the same with a red pile wavy; a Company (?) colour as Lt.-Colonel's but with a field gun or in the centre.

The Princess Ann of Danemark's Regiment (later 8th the King's Regiment). "Colonel's a dark pinkish crimson with Princess's cypher P A D with coronet in gold in the centre; Lr.-Colonel's the same but with a red cross of St. George bordered white with cypher and crown in the centre; Major's like Lt.-Colonel's but with a white pile wavy; 1st Captain's as Lt.-Colonel's but with numeral I in centre of first canton."

A set of drawings in the British Museum, Harl. MS. 6832, show the colours of Princess Anne's Regiment of Foot, Lord Ferrers Colonel. They are orange with red crosses edged white, but the MS. states they were changed to rose, cherry or pink. Earl Ferrers of Chartley raised the regiment in 1685, so these must be the first colours of the regiment. Colonel's colour orange, with gold coronet and cypher; Lt.-Colonel's orange with a red cross edged white; Major's the same with a white pile wavy, all three without any device; 1st Captain's as the Lt.-Colonel's but with the coronet and cypher; the 2nd with two cyphers and coronets side by side; the 3rd with three; the 4th with four arranged in a diamond; the 5th with five in the same arrangement; the 6th, 7th, 8th and 9th Captains with coronets and cyphers extending along the arms of the cross.

Colonel Francis Cornwall's (9th Foot). "Colonels plain orange; Lt.-Colonels orange with the Cross of St. George on a white square in the centre; Majors the same with a white pile wavy; 1st Captains the same as Lt.-Colonels but with a white roundel over top of the red cross."

Earl of Bath's (later 10th Foot). "Colonels plain light yellow; Lt.-Colonels yellow with a red cross bordered white; Major the same with a red pile wavy, 1st Captains as the Lt.-Colonels but with a suffle or organ rest in gold in the centre of the cross."

The Marquis of Worcester (later 11th Foot). "Colonel's crimson; Lt.-Colonel's crimson with a red cross bordered white; Major's the same with a white pile wavy. 1st Captain's as Lt.-Colonel's with a Portcullis and chains in gold in the centre of the cross."

The Duke of Norfolk's (later 12th Regiment). "Colonel's red with the crowned Lion stantant guardant on the Cap of Maintenance; Lt.-Colonel's with cross of St. George bordered white; Major's the same with the pile wavy; 1st Captain's as the Lt.-Colonel's but with a cross crosslet or fitché argent in the centre of the cross."

Earl of Huntingdon's (later 13th Foot). "Colonels plain yellow; Lt.-Colonels yellow with the cross bordered white; Majors the same with a red pile wavy; 1st Captains as Lt.-Colonels without any distinguishing device."

Sir Edward Hale's Regiment (14th Foot). "Colonels plain red; Lt.-Colonels red with St. George's cross bordered white with three flames or rays issuing from the angles of the cross; Majors the same but with a white pile wavy; 1st Captains as the Lt.-Colonels but with a white or silver ball in the centre of the cross."

Sir William Clifton's Regiment (15th Foot). "Colonels plain deep blueish green with the Clifton crest in the centre, out of a ducal coronet gules a demi-peacock pale argent and sable; Lt.-Colonels green with a St. George's cross bordered white with five white cinque-foils in each quarter; Majors the same with white pile wavy; 1st Captains the same as Lt.-Colonels but with the demi-peacock and coronet in the centre of the cross."

Colonel Buchan's Scotch Fusiliers (later 21st Foot). "Colonels white, in the centre a thistle with crown above, within the motto, 'Nemo me impune lacessit' in gold, the whole on a circular patch of blue; Lt.-Colonels blue with St. Andrew's cross in white, a single white ray or flame issuing from each of the angles of the cross; centre as the Colonels; the Majors the same as Lt.-Colonels with a red pile wavy; 1st Captains as Lt.-Colonels but with the numeral I in the upper canton."

From the bills, receipts, warrants and other papers in the Wardrobe Accounts much information has been found which fills in the gaps of long-standing. The references apply to the Household Troops and certain Royal regiments. Let us take the various notices of regiments in sequence:

1st Foot Guards.

1689. Aug. 6th. 24 colours of crimson and white taffeta, one of them (the Royal standard) to be embroidered on both sides with their Majestys' cypher and crown, having gold and silver tassels. The remaining 23 to be painted with their Majestys' cypher distinction and crown with 22 prs. of white and silver tassels. In the bill for the colours the tassels of the company colours are described as "silk gold and silver."

L

From the proportion of taffeta the colours were white with the crimson cross of St. George.

1692. The standard and Colonel's ensign have crimson and gold tassels. The ensigns' staves have gilt heads and the 23 ensigns are painted with badges and coronets. (? crowns).

1700. Nov. 27th. A crimson taffeta (the standard) with H.M.'s letters and crown embroidered in the centre, crimson silk and gold tassels and strings; one of crimson taffeta with a crown painted on each side with strings and tassels as above (the Colonel's ensign); one crimson and white in a cross with H.M.'s letters and crown painted both sides and a distinction of crimson colour for the Major's colour, crimson silk strings and tassels. Then follow three of the company colours with their badges. The next year six more company colours with the badges granted by Charles II.

Note: The standard was larger than the other colours.

1703. The standard was ordered to be increased in size and the company colours to be made three fingers larger every way. The standard tassels were all gold, the Colonel's crimson and gold and the remainder all crimson. The company colours were still white with the crimson cross.

1704. The standard as before, Colonel's ensign "a crown painted", Lt.-Colonel's cypher and crown, Major AR and crown with a "crimson blaze."

1706. The colour of H.M.'s company to be replaced, having been shot to pieces at the battle of Hochstett. This new standard was embroidered with the crown and cypher in the centre and the quarterly arms of the four kingdoms in the corners.

1707. The 24 colours with alteration in arms (owing to union with Scotland) issued.

1710 New colours for the Duke of Marlborough's company, the same, being shot to pieces at Blarignies. (Malplaquet.)

The 2nd or Coldstream Guards.

1690. June 23rd. Various company colours issued of crimson and white taffeta painted with their Majesties' cypher distinctions and crowns, silk and silver tassels and strings.

COLOURS

1692. The tassels for the Colonel's standard are crimson and gold and appears to have been larger. It is painted and gilded with very large cypher and crown and not embroidered, the company colours having lesser crowns and cyphers.

1695–6. This issue mentions for the first time "a very large Garter Starre and Crown" and 5 other colours to have garters and crowns and the 6 others badges and crowns.

Captain Balfour in his notes on the colours of the Foot Guards, by working out the quantities of red and white silk used in making the colours has come to the conclusion that the Colonel's ensign was plain white in 1692 and that it became crimson in 1695–6 when the Garter star was granted, and that the Royal standard and Colonel's ensign of the 1st Guards were crimson in 1695–6 and that there is no doubt that the Colonel's colour of the Coldstream Guards was crimson in 1700.

1700. Feb. 24th. Colours, 1 crimson taffeta with St. George's cross blaze and garter and crown over painted on each side, with crimson silk and gold tassels and strings (for the Colonel).

For the Lt.-Colonel 1 of crimson and white taffeta in a cross with St. George's cross blaze garter and crown painted on both sides. Strings and tassels as above.

For the Major crimson and white taffeta in a cross with St. George's Cross, blaze garter and crown over painted on each side, and a distinction of crimson taffeta in a quarter of the white, crimson silk tassels and strings; 1 of crimson and white taffeta in a cross, with a loop end and crown over, painted on each side. 1 as before with St. George on horseback and the dragon, crown above; 1 with a lion passant with crown over. (Warrants.)

1703. 12 colours. The Colonel's, Lt.-Colonel's and Major's as before; Captains' badges, lion and crown; feathers and crown; rose, garter and crown; panther and crown; centaur and crown; crossed swords and crown; crossed sceptres and crown; St. George and crown; knot within a garter and crown; all colours crimson and white; tassels crimson silk; Colonel's crimson and gold.

1707. 12 colours to be provided with the alteration in the arms upon the union with Scotland.

The Scots Guards

The 1691–96 entries for the 3rd Foot Guards refer to the Dutch Foot Guards and are recorded under that regiment. The Scots Guards were still on the Scottish establishment. See page 133.

1712. On the regiment being ordered to England we find ths first issue from the Great Wardrobe accounts. The Colonel's is crimson with crimson and gold tassels, the remaining colours to be the union with crimson silk tassels. The 18 ensigns to have their emblems, scrolls and mottoes painted on them. The Colonel's 'ane Lyon Rampant gules with a double treasure floured and counter flour'd 'En Ferus Hostis'; Lt.-Colonel's the Thistle and Rose from ye root 'Unita Fortior'; Major's ane Thistle withe Glory 'Nemo me impune lacesset'; 1st company Captains or a lyon seaseant guls holding in his dexter paw a sword, in the senister a skepter 'In Defence'; 2nd Co. a Lyon passant guls 'Timere nescius'; 3rd Co. a gryphon Rampant asur 'Belloque Ferox'; 4th a phœnix with flamis under and about her 'Per Funera Vitam'; 5th Jupiters Thunderbolt 'Horror ubique'; 6th a cannon fiering 'Concuss cadent urbes'; 7th a salamander surround'd with flamis 'Pascua nota mihi'; 8th asur, a saltyr or St. Andrew's cross argent, two colours thus painted with the different mottoes 'In hoc signo vinces' and 'Nemo me impune lacessit,' a trophy of arms 'Honoris refero,' a dog 'Intimera fide,' a bomb with its fuse in fire 'Terroram,' a Lyon rampant guls 'Intrepi das,' two colours thus painted and both the same motto, ane St. Andrew in the Glory with the Thistle 'Pendale,' 'nemo me impuni lacessit.' To add a crown to each of the above colours In white red and blue taffety 3 foot 11 inches long in broadness conforme. These are the colours of the 3rd regiment of Foot Guards under my command." (Signed.) Lothian.

Ensign tassels gold and crimson silk for the Colonels and crimson silk for the remainder.

"The devices of the Scots Guards are more correctly described," Captain Balfour says, "as warlike emblems than badges as in the case of the 1st and 2nd Foot Guards, as the Kings of Scotland did not have individual badges like the English sovereigns. These emblems were purely military and were not Scottish in character except those bearing the national arms."

It may be pointed out that all these colours were not issued during Queen Anne's reign, the remaining twelve being delivered in 1721. There is no mention of the pile wavy in these descriptions and it is believed it did not come into use until 1729, when it is mentioned in an issue of Scots Guards colours at that date. William III reduced the colours to three per regiment, although this order does not appear to have been always carried out, nor did it apply to the Foot Guards.

It has been suggested that the three colours were to be distributed as follows: one to the Grenadiers, Musketeers and Pikes, to this may be said that Grenadiers did not carry colours. In the Blenheim tapestries, however, the three colours are all grouped together in the centre of the regiment.

The Queen's Own Regiment of Marines, made marines in 1703 (later 4th King's Regiment), in 1702 were issued with twelve colours of which the following description appears in the Wardrobe accounts—fifteen Ells of white Taffata ¾ wide 14¾ ells of crimson. Received three colours viz., one of white with Queen's cypher and crown painted in gold on both sides for the Colonel, one of white and crimson in a cross, a crown on both sides for the Lt.-Colonel, one white and crimson in a cross with a blaze (pile wavy) for the Major: staves with gilt heads and brass ferules and pairs of crimson silk tassels and strings. In 1703 the remaining company colours were received, which were also of white and crimson with the following badges, all of which had the crown painted over them—a shaft of arrows, a Pomegranate, the feathers, a star, a wheatsheaf, a beacon, a half moon, a bull, a boar. The Queen's motto "Semper eadem" was to be painted on the colours and all had crimson tassels and strings, the whole bearing a close resemblance to Guards' colours with their red crosses and company badges.[1]

In 1707 "12 colours with alteration in arms" owing to the union with Scotland; this makes it appear that the colours were now Union flags.

The next and most valuable source of information is the MS book entitled *Les Triomphes du Roy Louis le Grand* in the Bibliothèque Nationale,

[1] These badges are interesting because they contain several not of common usage. The shaft of arrows is, as the Scots Brigade verse has it, "the Hollander's Arms"; the "Pomegranate" is the badge of Catherine of Aragon and the "feathers" could be the badge of Phillipa of Hainault, mother of the Black Prince, but in the Foot Guards this badge is given to Henry VI. The "star" and the "half moon" are two badges seen on the coin of Richard the First, but there is a certain amount of controversy as to whether the star is a "star" or a "sun." The beacon was used by Henry IV, a bull by Edward IV and a boar by Richard the Third, but the wheatsheaf, I cannot identify. The motto "Semper Eadem" was that used by Queen Elizabeth.

W. Y. CARMAN.

Paris. This contains coloured drawings of colours and standards captured by the French armies, together with name and year of the action in which they were taken.

The Rev. Percy Sumner, thanks to his knowledge of heraldy, has been able to attribute these to certain regiments by their Colonels' coats of arms or crests emblazoned on them; others unfortunately remain unidentifiable.

Landen, or Neerwinden, July 29th, 1693, a crimson colour with crowns in four corners, Colonel's ensign 1st Foot Guards. (Fig. 83 (a.))

A white St. Andrew's cross on blue field, Scots Guards.

Two white colours and one blue with thistle surrounded by a circle of R R's (=Royal Regt.) and W M's and motto *Nemo me impune lacessit*, Royal coat of arms in upper canton—Royal Scots. (Fig. 83 (b.))

One white colour, crown in centre surrounded by R R's and W M's and motto as above, thistle on the borders, the whole design in gold—Royal Scots. (Fig. 83 (e.))

Two dull yellow colours with St. George's cross edged white and a wavy saltire of crimson and black—3rd Foot (the Buffs). (Fig. 83 (d.))

Dixmude, July 26th, 1695.

Eight colours with Brewer's crest, out of a mural crown or, a hand grasping a battle axe argent (two being Majors' colours, three white, the rest St. George's cross on a white field (12th Foot). (Fig. 83 (g.))

Malplaquet 1709.

Two colours of the 3rd Foot (the Buffs) a union with cypher, W M and crown. These would, of course, be colours issued in the preceding reign and altered at the Union by adding the St. Andrew's cross but retaining the cypher of William and Mary. (Fig. 83 (e.))

Besides these there are a number of English and Scottish colours, some of which may be Dutch or belonging to the Scots Dutch regiments, the Dutch colours often having the Royal arms of England; as these are not generally known they are given below.

Fleurus, July 1st, 1690.

A crimson colour, in the centre a gauntletted hand holding a lance and issuing from a cloud, the device surrounded by a wreath of gold laurels, above on a silver scroll *Plustot Rompre Que Ploier*. In the upper canton a shield with arms of William III, in each of the other corners are piles wavy argent issuing from branches of gold laurels.

COLOURS

Dixmude, 1695.

A blue colour with white St. Andrew's cross, in each of the four angles of the cross are gold thistles. (It has been suggested that this may be a colour of the Scots Guards. (Fig. 83 (k.))

A dull yellow colour. In the centre a prancing white horse within a wreath of gold laurels; in each of the corners a gold thistle pointing inwards. No date or action given. (Fig. 83 (q.))

Tasnières (Malplaquet), 1709.

A blue colour having a large gold thistle in the centre surmounted by the crown and below on a white scroll *Nemo me impune lacessit*. (Fig. 83 (o.))

Bouchain, Oct. 19th, 1712.

A white colour, in the centre a shield with arms of England and Scotland, i.e. the three lions and the lion rampant, with the garter, the whole surmounted by the crown and encircled by a design of gold thistles with the circle of St. Andrew at the base, a blue ribbon edged gold and the motto *Munit et Ornat:* a small union in the upper canton. (Fig. 83 (l.))

Quesnoy, 1712.

A white St. Andrew's cross on a blue field, in the centre a gold thistle and crown with a red ribbon above with *Nemo me impune lacessit* (Fig. 83 (n.)).

Denin, July 24th, 1712.

A white colour having a shield with the Royal arms within the garter surmounted by the crown and the lion and unicorn supporters, below the unicorn the thistle and below the lion three roses proper, in the upper canton a small St. Andrew's cross on a blue field. (Fig. 83 (m.))

Two Scottish colours, one red and one blue, with a St. Andrew's cross throughout. No device.

The mention of Denin is curious unless it is an error, as there were no British units there, and it seems unlikely that even if they were units in foreign service they would have such a display of the Royal arms.

In Scotland the rules outlined by Venn do not appear to have been adopted. During the Civil War the colours bore the cross of St. Andrew over the whole flag, which was not necessarily blue, as the cross is found on a red field; colours like this are found later in the drawings of the trophies captured by the armies of Louis XIV.

The Colonel's colour was plain with his crest or motto, sometimes having the saltire in the upper canton.

(a) 1st Guards, 1693.   (b) 1st Foot, 1693.   (e) 1st Foot, 1693.   (d) 3rd Foot, 1693.

(e) 3rd Foot, 1709.   (f) 12th Foot, 1695.   (g) 12th Foot, 1695.   (h) Unidentified, 1688.

(i) Unidentified.   (k) Unidentified, 1695.   (l) Unidentified, 1712.   (m) Unidentified, 1712

(n) Unidentified, 1712.   (o) Unidentified, 1709.   (p) Unidentified.   (q) Unidentified, c. 1700.

FIG. 83. Colours of Foot Regiments, 1688–1712.

COLOURS

The Pile wavy is not seen until after the Restoration, but this was by no means the invariable rule.

The Company Captains' colours were largely distinguished by numerals, but spots and devices were sometimes used in the same way as in England.

In an article on Colours in the *Journal of the Royal United Service Institution*, a blue colour is reproduced. In the upper canton is the St. George's Cross with three white piles wavy issuing from the lower corner and passing across the entire flag.

It is said to have been born by one of Monmouth's regiments during the rebellion, but it appears more probably to have been a company colour of a regular or militia unit. It is identical in design to those of the London Train Bands of 1642.

It remained in the possession of the same family for over two hundred years.

A colour carried by a foot regiment at the landing of William III at Torbay is of blue silk with the St. George's Cross in the upper canton and having three Pascal Lambs placed diagonally across it. The Ensign who carried it was billeted at the house of a Mr. John Chappell at Newton Abbott, where he fell ill and was unable to follow the army when it advanced. His illness increased and he finally died, his sash and the colour remaining in the possession of Chappell and his descendants ever since until it was bequeathed to the Royal United Service Institution, where it can still be seen, in a perfect state of preservation. (Fig. 83 (h.))

Much ceremonial was observed in handling the "colours" and old books on the art of War devote considerable space to the manner in which they were to be waved and flourished. This was, apparently, an old custom and the Lansquenets, in particular, prided themselves on the expert way they flourished their ensigns. Elton in his *Complete Body of the Art Military* published in 1659 and Captain Thomas Venn have much to say on the subject.

John Blackwell in his *Compendium of Military Discipline as it is practised by the Honourable Artillery Company*, published in 1726, gives the various flourishes and waves which are really a revised version of those given by Venn. He heads his chapter with "General Rules to be observed by Ensigns" of which the following is a resumé:

1. When the colours were brought to the Parade they were to be carried in the right hand "the end of the staff against the waist, the back of the hand over the staff, the elbow extended, sheet flying and the left hand against the side" (Fig. 84).

2. The colours on being "lodged or dislodged should always be attended by a guard."

3. Only the Ensign to handle the colours.

4. When the Ensign was at the hind or front of his company he was to carry them flying as in No. 1 "or display them to and fro in a direct circle changing from hand to hand and no more and to take post 12 foot before the front."

FIG. 84. Ensign, 1688.

5. "On the long march" the colours were to be carried as in No 1 "or if the march be long, on the right shoulder, as high as you can, your elbow close to your side and the sheet flying but on going through a gate way carry your colours against your wast ported."

6. "When the drum beats a preparative to draw up your company, show your readiness by advancing your colours upright, with half outstretched arm, before you, and hand as high as your breast."

7. Especial care was to be taken not to disgrace the colours "which some do" by "levelling them as with a halbert to dress the ranks."

8. In saluting General or Field officers while on the march the colours to be carried flying and "against the waist ported, and whether the General be on the right or left when within 6 paces of him give your

sheet a flourish turn over your staff to the hand he is of without any halting and pursue your march with your spear within two foot of the ground, and take off your hat with your left hand at the same time, and bring it smartly down the full length of your arm close by your side keeping straight and bold aspect, without bowing head or body, when six paces beyond the officer saluted, raise the colour to its former posture and return your hat on your head." (Fig. 85).

FIG. 85. Ensign, 1680.

9. "When the General marches to review and is to be saluted from order, then your sheet being held to your wast, flying, when he is advanced within 6 paces, give your sheet a flourish, turn over the staff to the right (as it is usual for him to march from the angle of the front of the regiment or battalion) and spread your colours on the ground and take off your hat as before without bowing, continue in that posture until he has past you six paces then raise your sheet to its former posture and return your hat" (Fig. 85).

10. "When the Company or Regiment is drawn up and any General or noble stranger . . . you ought to wave your colours and bow the head of them as they pass by, and at same time make a small bow of your body."

11. When the Company ground arms the colours are never to be laid on the ground or placed in unworthy hands but to be tied "upright in a stand made with a triangle of halberts at the front of the Company."

12. When the Company is ordered to troop off the colours to be furled and carried advanced in the right hand.

The author of this book then goes on to describe the "8 flourishes of the colours, which formerly were very much in use, but of late years it has been laid aside, however I shall mention and describe them, in order to raise an emulation in the ensign bearers to revive the practice."

1. "In the change of your colours with a plain wave from hand to hand over your hand."
2. "In the change of your colours with lofty turns over your hand, from hand to hand, each hand performing their turns from right to left, and from left to right before you deliver them."
3. "In the bringing of your colours with a wave and lofty turn over your head, down on your left shoulder, lifting up your colours, which being done three times in the same manner, you deliver them into your left hand to be performed from the right shoulder as before."
4. "Is the same as the last figure, only with your left hand you give your sheet an off-turn flourish before you, which done three times, you deliver it into the left hand to be performed in like manner.
5. "Is with the right hand with lofty turns, you bring your staff under your left arm, at the same time claping your left hand over your right arm on the butt-end of your staff, raise them up quick again, and being done three times deliver your colours into your left hand to exercise in the same manner.
6. "Is with lofty turns in your right hand, bring your staff down on your left shoulder, raise it up quick, and bring it down on your right shoulder, and wheel it once, in the like manner, bring it from your left shoulder to the right, and wheel it twice and so a third time, and then deliver it into left hand to be performed in like manner.
7. "Is with your right hand after lofty turns over your head, you bring your sheet before you, and with your left hand against the butt-end of your staff, you give your sheet one wave before you, and raise it again, and bring it down again, and give it two brisk waves or turns before you, and being raised up, bring it down a third time, and wave it three times as before, and thus to be done in like manner with your left hand.
8. "Do the lofty turns of your sheet with your right hand, in the form of a figure 8 which done three times, you deliver your colour into your left hand to be performed in like manner."

These waves and flourishes were also used as a means of drilling infantry. Marlborough is mentioned as highly approving the system.

This system of signals is said to have been devised by Captain William Burrell of the 1st Foot Guards about 1707. In 1737 at 6 o'clock on July 10th Colonel Pulteney exercised "seven Battalions of the Guards by the wave of

COLOURS

the colours as usual when the King sees them."
Unfortunately there is no mention of the various
flourishes used for the different drill movements.

Elton says that "when any commander or
souldier of worth shall be deceased and when
the corpse is brought into the street, the Pikes
and Musketiers being ranged in double files
facing in inwards, are properly assembled . . .
in the next place the ensign strips the colours
off from his staffe and ties them round his waist,
putting a black ribbon towards the very end of
his staffe, he after faceth the body of Pikes standing in the rear of them, trailing his staffe in the
same posture. Afer which (the interment) being
over and the vollies fired the ensign may put his
colours upon his staffe and furl them up."

FIG. 86. Ensign, 1688.

STANDARDS AND GUIDONS

Standards and guidons were embroidered and had fringes of gold or silver
or gold and silver intermixed with coloured silk and having cords and tassels
of the same colours. The fact that standards and guidons were embroidered
necessitated their being made of double silk damask. They were carried on a
pole, which was made exactly like the old tilting lance of the Middle Ages.
It was made with vertical grooves and had a long metal bar or staple fixed to
the side. To this was attached the swivel clasp on the colour belt. It must be
presumed that there was some kind of leather socket attached to the stirrup
for the foot of the pole to rest in.[1]

Cavalry standards were called cornets, as were the officers who carried
them. Dragoons originally used the title of Ensign for the officer carrying
their guidon, but later changed it to Cornet like the cavalry.

The earliest known post Restoration cavalry standard is that of the Scots
Troop of Life Guards, now in the Scottish National Naval and Military
Museum, Edinburgh. For many years previously it had been in the Palace of
Holyroodhouse. It measures about 27 inches by 25 and is made of crimson
silk damask heavily embroidered with gold and silver on both sides, with the
thistle and rose, having either side the C R of the Royal cypher and sur-

[1] See p. 155.

FIG. 87.
Standard. Scots Troop
of Life Guards, 1662.

mounted by the crown. The scroll, or ribbon, bears the motto *Dieu et Mon Droit*, and below are three smaller crowns representing the other kingdoms of the realm. The fringe is of gold and silver intermixed and is three inches deep. This standard was probably given to the Troop raised, or rather re-raised, in 1660–1.

Nathan Brooks describes the standards and guidons of the regiments present at the review on Putney Heath in 1684 as follows:

"The King's Own Troop of Life Guards and Troop of Horse Grenadiers: the standard crimson with the Royal cypher and crown. The guidon differenc'd only from the standard by being rounded and slit at the ends.

"The Queen's Troop and Horse Grenadiers the standard and guidon as the King's.

"The Dukes (of York) Troop and Horse Grenadiers, the standard and guidon of yellow damask with His Highnesses cypher and crown.

"The Regiment of Horse Guards (The Blues) The standard of the King's Troop crimson with the imperial crown embroidered; the Colonel's Troop the Royal cypher on crimson. The Major's gold streams on crimson; 1st Troop the Rose crowned, 2nd a thistle crowned, 3rd a flower de luce crowned, 4th the harp crowned, 5th the Royal Oak, all embroidered on crimson colours.

"The King's own Royal Regiment of Dragoons commanded by John Lord Churchill. The colours of each Troop thus distinguished—The Colonel's the Royal cypher and crown embroidered on crimson. The Lt.-Colonel's the Rays of the sun proper crowned issuing out of a cloud, a badge of the Black Prince. 1st Troop the top of a beacon crowned or with flames of fire proper, a badge of Henry V. 2nd Troop two estreages (ostrich) feathers crowned, argent, a badge of Henry VI. 3rd a Rose and Pomegranate impaled, leaves and stalk vert, a badge of Henry VIII. 4th a Phœnix in flames proper, a badge of Queen Elizabeth each embroidered on crimson."

The following description of the standards of the Queen's Regiment of Horse (1st Dragoon Guards) is taken from the Wardrobe accounts—"8 standards of crimson damask with gold and silver fringes tassels and strings;

embroidered on both sides viz., 1st or Colonels standard two C's under our Royal crown. 2nd or Lt.-Colonels our Royal crown. 3rd or Majors our Royal crest. 4th or Queen's Troop the Rose and Crown. 5th fleur de lys and crown. 6th Thistle and crown. 7th Harp and crown. 8th plain without a fringe.

"Trumpet banners of the same colour and fringes etc. with our Royal arms on both sides. The Kettle Drum banners embroidered as our dearest consort's Troop of Guards are."

Sandford's description of the standards and guidons is our next source of information with the drawings in the Colour Book in Windsor Castle. Beginning with the Life Guards the 1st Troop "had a cornet of crimson damask" doubled being 2 foot 6 inches flying and 2 foot 3 inches on the staff, was fringed about with silver and gold intermixed, three inches deep, with strings and tassels suitable, and in the middle was embroidered the King's cypher ensign'd with a large Imperial crown of gold within a scroll of silver, where on the King's motto viz., *Dieu et mon droit*, was wrought in black silk; and under the scroll three lesser Imperial crowns of gold were embroidered.

The Guidon was also crimson damask made up and embroidered in all respects as the cornet from which it differed only in form, having a forked tail, to the points whereof from the staff it was about a yard and 3 inches flying.

The 2nd Troop. Their cornet of white damask doubled being 2 ft. 6 inches flying and as much in depth upon the staff was fringed about with gold and silver 3 inches deep with strings and tassels suitable and in the middle was imbroidered the King's cypher ensigned with an imperial crown of gold sustained by two angels of silver, that on the right side having a sword in his hand and that on the left a Palm branch: under the cypher was the year of our Lord 1685 wrought in figures of gold and below the said figures a scroll of gold with the words *Dieu et mon Droit* in black silk and under the scroll the three lesser imperial crowns of gold.

The Guidon was of the same silk made up and embroidered as the cornet, differing from it only in form, having a forked tail, being 3 foot 3 inches from the staff.

3rd Troop—Their cornet of yellow damask doubled being 2 feet 6 inches square, was fringed about with gold and silver panel, three inches deep with strings and tassels suitable and in the middle was embroidered the King's cypher of silver ensigned with a large imperial crown of gold within a scroll also of silver whereon the King's motto *Dieu et mon Droit* wrought in gold and under the scroll three lesser Imperial crowns of gold.

The Guidon was also of yellow damask in all respects as the cornet etc. . . . and from the staff about a yard 3 inches flying.

It is curious that the Life Guards being regiments of Horse should have a guidon as well as a standard, the latter being typical for Dragoons.

In 1661 only one cornet was posted to each Troop of Life Guards. In 1674 a second cornet or guidon was appointed, were it not for the fact that both these, the standard and cornet, were carried in each Troop up to 1787, one might have thought that the guidon was for the Grenadier Troop.

In the troops of Horse Grenadiers a guidon was also carried up to their disbandment in 1788.

After Sandford's description of the Household cavalry standard at James II's coronation let us give a brief summary of those in the Colour Book of the same date.

The Royal Regiment of Horse commanded by the Earl of Oxford, later called the Oxford Blues to distinguish it from the Dutch Guards of William III.

It had the privilege of bearing Royal badges, granted by the King in 1661. Some of these have been described by Nathan Brooks, but the regiment having been augmented by additional Troops since that time, further badges had been granted.

The standards are all of crimson damask with gold and crimson fringes, tassels and cords.

The King's Troop had the cypher J R surmounted by the crown and above this a silver label with the motto *Dieu et mon Droit* and the three smaller crowns below, as on the standard of the Life Guards. (Fig. 88).

The Colonel's the Royal crest of the crown surmounted by the crowned lion *passant guardant or.*

The remaining Troops' standards were emblazoned with the following badges surmounted by the crown, viz: the Lt.-Colonel's the rose or; a thistle or; a fleur de lis; a gold harp with silver strings; a gold oak tree; a gold portcullis; and the badge of the garter, i.e. the red cross of St. George within the blue garter. (Fig. 88).

The Queen's Majesty's Horse (1st Dragoon Guards) are represented by three standards in the Colour Book; the Colonel's yellow damask, in the

The Royal Regiment of Dragoons, 1685.
Fig. 88. Cavalry Standards, 1685.

centre the Queen's cypher M B E R interlaced in gold surmounted by the crown. The Lt.-Colonel's and the Captains' the same and all having black and gold fringes and tassels.

The Earl of Peterborrow's Horse (2nd Dragoon Guards) all three of plain white damask without any device fringes and tassels silver and yellow.

The Earl of Plymouth's Horse (3rd Dragoon Guards) all three of plain green damask with fringes and tassels of green and silver.

[153]

M

The Earl of Thanet's Horse (disbanded in William III's reign). Blue damask fringed and tassels blue and silver. The Colonel's: In the centre a silver sea lion sejeant (the crest of the Tufton family) on a wreath of black and silver surmounted by the Earl's coronet. (Fig. 88). The Lt.-Colonel's and the 1st Captain's quite plain, the latter having the numeral 1 in the upper corner near the pole.

The Earl of Arran's Horse (4th Dragoon Guards) the Colonel's white damask with crimson and gold fringes and tassels, with the Hamilton crest in the centre, viz. on a mount vert an oak tree fructed and penetrated by a saw, the wreath red and silver, the whole surmounted by a silver scroll with motto "Through." (Fig. 88). The other standards quite plain.

The Earl of Shrewsbury's Horse (5th Dragoon Guards) the Colonel's yellow damask, fringe and tassels silver and yellow. In the centre, a lion rampant argent (an armorial bearing of the Talbot family). (Fig. 88). The other standards were quite plain.

The Princess Ann of Denmark's Horse (disbanded 1692). Crimson damask with gold and crimson fringe and tassels. In the centre the Princess's cypher P A D in gold surmounted by her coronet. (vide

All three standards are exactly the same.

The Queen Dowager's Horse (6th Dragoon Guards). All three standards are alike, being of green damask with green and gold fringes and tassels, and with the cypher two C's interlaced surmounted by a crown (vide

The Royal Regiment of Dragoons (1st Royal Dragoons) of 8 Troops each having a guidon of crimson damask with fringes and tassels of crimson and silver, each with a Royal badge surmounted by a gold crown. Some of these badges were described by Nathan Brooks, but not ascribed to the same Troops. The Colonel's; the late King's cypher two gold C's interlaced. The Lt.-Colonel's; a gold escarbuncle (a badge of Henry II.) 1st Captains' two silver ostrich feathers in saltire; 2nd rose and pomegranate impaled leaves and stalk vert (a badge of Henry VIII); 3rd, the rays of the sun issuing from a cloud (a badge of the Black Prince); 4th the beacon and flames (badge of Henry V); 5th a tiger passant guardant on a mount vert, spotted with roundels alternately black, yellow and red, and flames of fire issuing from its mouth (a badge of Henry VI); 6th a phœnix in flames (a badge of Queen Elizabeth). (Fig. 88).

The Queen's Majesty's Dragoons (3rd Hussars).

COLOURS

The Colonel's pinkish crimson damask with the Queen's cypher M B E R in gold with crown above, fringe and tassels gold and crimson. The Lt.-Colonel's the same and the Captains' without the cypher.

The Princess Ann of Denmark's Dragoons (4th Hussars). All three guidons of perfectly plain yellow damask with silver and yellow fringe and tassels.

The following descriptions come from the bills, etc., in the Great Wardrobe Accounts.

The Life Guards. 2nd Troop of Horse Grenadiers.

1689. "2 large standards of white damask embroidered on both sides with their Majesties cypher and crown, with gold fringes tassels and strings. Standard belts and boot leathers." These last would be the bucket or socket for the base of the pole to rest in.

"1st and 3rd Troops of Horse Guards 2 standards of crimson and 2 of yellow damask with gold and silver fringes and tassels."

"For the 3 Troops 2 standards of red 2 of white and 2 of yellow damask all embroidered with cyphers and crowns in gold and silver; with gold and silver tassels as hath been accustomed."

1702. "6 standards for three troops of (Life) Guards of crimson white and green damask (i.e. the 1st, 2nd, and 3rd Troops respectively) with gold tassels, the iron work of the cornet staves all gilt."

"For the troop of Horse Grenadiers 1 guidon richly embroidered on both sides with H.M.'s crown and cypher for the 3 Troops of Horse Guards. For embroidering 3 square standards and 3 guidons being crimson white and green with Her Majesty's cypher and crown and motto *Semper eadem* on both sides."

1706. "1 standard of blue damask for 1st Troop of Horse Grenadiers; embroidered with H.M.'s cypher and crown and having gold fringe and tassels."

1712. "1st Troop of Horse Grenadiers a blue guidon embroidered with Rose and Thistle crown and scroll on both sides, gold tassels and fringe. The 2nd or Scots Troop as the 1st but on crimson damask."

1713. "1st Troop of Horse Guards a standard and guidon embroidered with a Rose Thistle crown and scrolls both alike upon crimson damask. 2 prs rich gold tassels."

"2nd Troop as above but on white Damask. The 3rd on yellow and the 4th or Scots Troop on blue."

From the foregoing the change in the design will be noticed, due to the Union with Scotland.

1689. "For the Earl of Oxford's Horse a crimson damask standard embroidered both sides with their Majesties cypher surmounted with Imperial crown, with scrolls and 3 lesser crowns, with gold and silver fringe, etc., all as the 1st Troop of Horse Guards."

1690. "For embroidering richly a standard with their Majesties crown and cypher on both sides, a cornet staff all gilt with belt and boot leather."

1693. "Standard with same devices as 1689."

1704. "Crimson damask for 9 standards, gold fringe and tassels. Her Majesty's cypher and crown in gold and silver on both sides."

1708. "9 standards with alterations in H.M.'s arms. The Queen's Regiment of Horse (1st Dragoon Guards)."

1692. "9 standards of crimson damask embroidered both sides with their Majesties cypher and crown, fringed with silver and tassels and strings of crimson and silver, gilt swivels and sockets."

The MS book of the trophies of Louis XIV gives sketches of the following cavalry standards and guidons:

Landen or Neerwinden July 29th, 1693.

A crimson standard with M R—Queen's Horse (1st Dragoon Guards). A yellow standard with M R of the same regiment.

Dixmude, July 26th, 1695.

Two plain blue guidons fringed with gold The Queen's (3rd Dragoons).

A blue guidon with gold tassels and fringe. In the centre a rose and thistle with a scroll below and crown above with a smaller crown in each corner. This is said to come from MS book, but no date or battle is given.

The standards of the 4th or Dutch Troop of Life Guards are described in the Great Wardrobe Accounts—

1689, Oct. "For richly embroidering 2 standards with their Majesties cyphers and crown on both sides £30 and again 2 colours (standards) of blue damask trimmed with gold and silver fringe and large strings and tassels." The embroidery as described above. "2 standard staves with belts and boot leathers."

1696. The standards are similarly described.

[156]

COLOURS

BADGES OF THE FOOT GUARDS

Grenadier Guards—each badge is ensigned with Imperial Crown.

1st Company. The Royal Crest; crowned lion on crown.
Granted in 1661 by Charles II.

2nd Company. Badge of Henry VIII; a Rose Gules, surmounted by another Argent, barbed and seeded proper.
Granted in 1661 by Charles II.

3rd Company. Royal Badge of Henry V; a Fleur de lis or.
Granted in 1661 by Charles II.

4th Company. Royal Badge of Henry VII; a Portcullis with chains, pendant or.
Granted in 1661 by Charles II.

5th Company. Royal Badge of Edward IV; the Sun in its Splendour Or, thereon a Rose Argent, barbed and seeded proper.
Granted in 1661 by Charles II.

6th Company. Badge of Scotland; a Thistle stalked and leaved proper.
Granted in 1661 by Charles II.

7th Company. The Badge of Ireland; a Harp or stringed Argent.
Granted in 1661 by Charles II.

8th Company. The Badge of Wales as borne by Henry VII; on a Mount vert a Dragon passant with wings elevated Gules.
Granted in 1661 by Charles II.

9th Company. The Royal Badge of Henry VII; on a Mount vert, a Greyhound Passant Argent, gogged with a Collar Gules studded and ringed Or.
Granted in 1661 by Charles II.

10th Company. The Royal Badge of Richard II; the Sun in its Splendour Or.
Granted in 1661 by Charles II.

11th Company. The Royal Badge of James I; an Unicorn passant Argent, armed, maned tufted and unguled Or, gorged with a Princes Coronet and the Chain reflexed over the back of the last.
Granted in 1661 by Charles II.

12th Company. The Royal Badge of King Henry IV; on a Mount Vert an Antelope statant Argent, attired, tufted, ducally gorged and chain reflexed over the back Or.
Granted in 1661 by Charles II.

13th Company. Royal Badge of King Richard II; on a Mount Vert. A Hart couchant Argent attired unguled, ducally gorged and Chain reflexed over the back Or.

Granted in 1666 by Charles II.

14th Company. Royal Badge of Edward IV; a Falcon with wings expanded Argent; beaked, legged and belled Or, within a Fetterlock closed of the last.

Granted in 1666 by Charles II.

15th Company. Royal Badge of Henry IV; a Rose Gules barbed and seeded Or.

Granted in 1666 by Charles II.

16th Company. Royal Badge of Henry IV; on a Mount Vert a Swan with wings expanded Argent beaked and legged Gules ducally gorged and chain reflexed over the back Or.

Granted in 1666 by Charles II.

17th Company. Badge of Anne Bullen, 2nd wife of Henry VIII; a Falcon wings elevated Argent, crowned and holding in the dexter Talon a Sceptre Or, standing on the Trunk of a Tree eradicated, from the dexter side thereof sprouting a branch of white and red Roses barbed and seeded proper.

Granted in 1666 by Charles II.

18th Company. Royal Badge of Edward III; the Trunk of a Tree couped and erased Or, from the dexter and sinister sides, three leaves sprouting vert.

Granted in 1666 by Charles II.

19th Company. A Sceptre in bend dexter Or, surmounted by a Sword in bend sinister proper, Pommel and Hilt of the first.

Granted in 1666 by Charles II.

20th Company. On a Mount Vert an Oak Tree, therein a Man's Face Imperially Crowned all proper (allusive to the preservation of King Charles after Worcester).

Granted in 1666 by Charles II.

21st Company. The Royal Badge of Edward III; the Sun rising Or, behind Clouds proper.

Granted in 1713 by Queen Anne.

22nd Company. The Royal Badge of Henry V; a Beacon Or, fired proper.

Granted in 1713 by Queen Anne.

COLOURS

23rd Company. The Royal Badge of Henry VI; two Ostrich Feathers in saltire Argent, quilled Or, the dexter surmounted by the sinister.

Granted in 1713 by Queen Anne.

24th Company. The Crest of Ireland; on a Wreath Or and Azure a Tower triple towered of the first, from the Portal a Hart springing Argent, attired and unguled Or.

Granted in 1713 by Queen Anne.

25th Company. On a Shield Argent the Cross of St. George.

Granted in 1854 by Queen Victoria.

26th Company. The Arms of Nassau as borne by King William the Third; Azure billetee and Lion rampant Or.

27th Company. The Badge of the Most Honourable Military Order of the Bath as established in 1727, Or.

Granted in 1854 by Queen Victoria.

28th Company. The Crest of Brunswick or Hanover; out of a Ducal Coronet a Pillar Proper the top adorned with a Coronet and Plume of three Peacocks Feathers Proper charged with a Star Argent on either side of the Pillar out of the Coronet a sickle Argent handles Gules the backs adorned with small tufts of Peacocks feathers and between the sickles before the Pillar a Horse courant argent.

Granted in 1854 by Queen Victoria.

29th Company. The Union Badge of Ireland; a Trefoil Vert.

Granted in 1854 by Queen Victoria.

30th Company. The Crest of Prince Albert; out of a Ducal Coronet a Pillar of the Arms of Saxony crowned with a like Coronet and thereon a plume of three peacocks feathers proper.

Granted in 1854 by Queen Victoria.

COLDSTREAM GUARDS:

1st Company. On a Mount Vert, a Lion sejeant guardant, his tail passed between his legs and reflexed over his back, argent.

Granted by William III, 1696.

2nd Company. Badge of Prince of Wales. Three Feathers, Argent, quilled Or, out of a Prince's Coronet, Or.

Granted by William III, 1696.

3rd Company. On a Mount vert, Henry VI, a Panther Guardant, Argent, spotted sable, azure and gules, and sending forth flames of fire proper from the mouth and ears.

Granted by William III, 1696.

4th Company. Two Swords in saltire, with the points upwards, argent, hilts and pommets Or.

5th Company. St. George slaying the Dragon, all proper.

6th Company. Henry IV of Lancaster. A Rose gules seeded Or barbed vert, within the Garter.

7th Company. Royal Badge of Stephen on a Mount Vert, a Sagittari proper.

8th Company. Two Sceptres in saltire, Or.

9th Company. Badge of Richard II. The Knot of the Collar of the Garter Order Or, within the Garter.

10th Company. An Escarbuncle, Or.

11th Company. Badge of Richard the Third on a Mount Vert, a Boar Passant, Argent, armed tusked and bristled, Or.

12th Company. On a Mount Vert, a Dun Cow.

13th Company. A Badge of Henry VIII. A Rose Gules surmounted by another Argent, barbed and seeded proper, empaled with a Pomegranate Or, stalked proper.

14th Company. On a Mount Vert, a Horse courant, Argent.

15th Company. The Crown of Charlemegne, all proper.

All the above badges granted by William III, 1696.

16th Company. Badge as 28th Company of Grenadier Guards.

Granted in 1814 by George III. (Was as 19th Company.)

17th Company. The Royal and Imperial Monogram of Queen Victoria in gold. Granted 1901.

18th Company. Henry VI. On a Mount Vert, an Heraldic Tiger Argent armed, unguled, tufted, ducally gorged and chain reflexed over back, Or.

19th Company. The Badge of Henry IV. A Rose Gules seeded Or, barbed Vert within a Garter of the Order of the Garter, with the George appendant all proper.

20th Company. A representation of the lesser George, of the Garter, Or encircled with the Garter and motto in their proper colours.

21st Company. William II. An Eagle wings expanded sable, beaked and legged or with a glory around its head Or.

COLOURS

22nd Company. Two Laurel Branches in saltire, Vert, enfiled with the circle of the Imperial Crown proper.

23rd Company. Crest of George Monk, Duke of Albemarle. On a Chapeau Gules turned up Ermine, a Cat-a-mountain statant guardant, per pale sable and argent between two branches of Broom Vert, fructed proper.

24th Company. The crest of Duke of Cambridge. A Lion statant guardant upon the circle of the coronet of H.R.H. with the like coronet on its head, all Or. The Lion charged on the Breast with a label of 3 points Argent, the centre point charged with St. George's Cross and each of the others with two hearts in pale gules.

All the above badges were granted by Queen Victoria in 1901.

ARTILLERY

THE Artillery was on a somewhat different footing to the rest of the army, being under the direct administration of the Master-General of Ordnance and all Artillery and Engineer Officers' commissions were signed by him.

During this period there was, practically speaking, no regular corps of artillery with the exception of a few master gunners and their mates, who regarded themselves as specialists.

In the case of war what was called a train of artillery was formed by the Master of Ordnance. This comprised men, guns, horses and specialists besides the artillery and engineer officers. At the conclusion of the campaign the train was disbanded. A train would consist of the following:

A Comptroller
A Commissary of artillery
A Paymaster of the train
A Waggon master
A Commissary of draught horses
3 Gentlemen of ordnance
A Purveyor (Quartermaster)
Provost Marshal
Master gunner and two mates

a surgeon, tent keeper, farrier, Master carpenter, Master wheelwright, Master collar-maker, Master cooper. These would all have their assistants, and besides these there would be 32 gunners, 32 matrosses (or gunners' assistants), their duty being to see after all gun tackle, the actual charging, laying and firing being the duty of the gunner.

Six conductors (these were assistants to the Commissary of stores to conduct depots and magazines from place to place and had also care of the ammunition waggons in the field). 118 carters, 1 kettle drummer, 22 Pioneers, the engineer officer and a *petardier*, who commanded the mortar detachment which consisted of 4 to 19 firemasters, 4 to 30 bombardiers. The firemasters who seem to have had the duty of making explosives for the destruction of city gates, bridges, etc., would complete the personnel.

The guns for such a "trayne" would consist of brass pieces of various calibres—18 pounders, 6 pounders, demi culverins, sakers and minions.

The carters were civilians and together with their horses would be contracted for, but, even so, in some instances at least, they were given a distinctive dress while serving with the army. The presence of such a proportion of civilians together with the gunners, hastily assembled, whose only duty being to serve the guns but otherwise having little or no military training or discipline, was no doubt the reason for raising the Ordnance Regiment with the title of "My Royal Regiment of Fusiliers,"[1] so that besides acting as an escort to the guns on the line of march it would be a trained and disciplined body of men in case of panic among the hastily organised Train. James II's Warrant of 1685 for the raising of the regiment mentions 100 aprons per coy. of 100 men. From this it would seem that they were expected to do a certain amount of work with the guns, which would have included

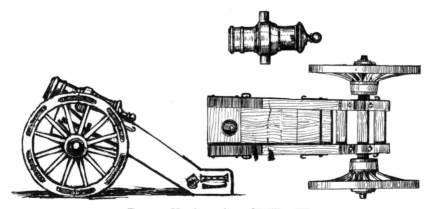

FIG. 90. Howitzer, time of William III.

[1] And in Scotland a similar corps, the Royal Scots Fusiliers.

handling the chevaux de frise and other defences. The purpose, therefore, of these aprons seems to have been to protect the men's regimentals. No doubt after the Train had been on service for any considerable time owing to a prolonged campaign it would attain a considerable degree of steadiness.

The horses were harnessed tandem-wise to the light field pieces, but in the case of the heavy siege guns they would be in pairs so as to avoid the space

Fig. 91. The Royal Regiment of Fusiliers, 1685.

that would be taken up on the road by a long team of animals; the wheeler, however, would be in single harness in the shafts. The drivers mostly marched on foot beside their teams, one by the leader and the other by the wheeler. In some prints the drivers are shown riding. The harness would be the ordinary farm wagon type in use at the time.

The Train had a pair of kettle drums mounted on a four-wheeled carriage with seats for the drummer and driver. These drums went with the army to Ireland and also to the Continent during the campaigns of William III and the Spanish Succession, and also took part in the funeral procession of the Duke of Marlborough.

Their drum banners were crimson damask embroidered with the Sovereign's coat of arms. The pair now hang in the R.A. Mess at Woolwich, the coat of arms being that of George I.

In the Tower is a set of contemporary models of Marlborough's Train showing guns, pontoons, wagons, field forges and finally the kettle drum carriage. All these vehicles are painted a dark green, but that this was the original colouring is by no means certain as gun carriages on the Continent at that time and for long after were generally painted red. In the painting of Tangier some heavy siege guns are shown, one is painted a faded red colour and the others grey.

It is now time to turn to the dress of the personnel of the Train. In 1662 we find from an inventory of clothing for the "Trayne" in Scotland that the gunner's coat was "fine scarlet cloth laced with black velvet as the Yeomen of the Guard at London embroidered with a thistle and crown and two cannons on the breast and one on the back and gunner's badges of silver."

It has been stated that these badges were a metal or cloth St. Andrew's cross worn on the right breast or arm.

For the same train in 1683 we find six suits of fine scarlet cloth lined with serge, long silk loops, silver buttons, buff belts with silver buckles, buff gloves, furred caps laced with gold galloon, scarlet stockings and halberds. For the under gunners "six suits so laced, with stockings, caps, buff belts with steel buckles and bearing the King's name on their grenado bags, patronashes and bagonettes."

About 1685 Lt.-General Drummond was empowered to import red cloth from England for the dress of the Artillery.

From the above it appears that the gunners wore caps similar to those of the grenadiers and dragoons. The *London Gazette* also states that "the gunners of the garrison of Tangier had lately appeared in their new livery coats and caps."

FIG. 92. Kettle Drum Carriage, 1705.

A train under the orders of the Earl of Feversham in 1685 was equipped as follows:

"2 Gunners Mates and 32 Gunners, each a field stave or linstock.

"32 Matrosses each a half pike, hanger and belt.

"The Pioneer Sergeant a partizan, hanger and belt.

"The Pioneer Corporal a halberd, hanger and belt.

"20 Pioneers each a hanger and belt and either a spade, a shovel, or pick and were dressed in red jackets and red caps.

"A Drummer with his drum, hanger and belt.

"The Artificers wore red clothes laced.

"The Conductors, wheelers, carpenters, coopers, smiths and collarmakers each a hanger and belt."

This train was, however, so deficient of draught animals that the Bishop of Winchester, who it is stated was with the Royal forces, lent his coach horses to help drag the guns into position at the Battle of Sedgemoor. This was Peter Mews, who had been Bishop of Bath and Wells and had formerly served as an officer in Holland and Scotland. Nor was it only horses that seem to have been lacking, as Sergeant Weems of Dunbarton's Royal Regiment of Foot appears to have acted as gunner. A Warrant February 26th, 1685 directs that he "should be paid forty pounds for good service in the action at Sedgemoor in firing the great guns against the rebels."

In 1688 on the arrival of William of Orange in England a train was formed, the personnel attached to it being dressed as follows:

The Pioneers red cloth coats and red kersey breeches, leather montreur caps, woollen stockings, shoes and buckles and neck cloth.

The Matrosses striped jackets and breeches, leather caps, blue stockings, shoes and buckles, their arms being half pikes and hangers. This striped material sounds as if it were ticken similar to that issued to seamen at this period and, if so, was possibly white striped with red. It seems probable that this was a kind of undress clothing.

The Conductors had red cloth cloaks and the Chief Engineer was provided with a suit of silk armour.

It may be as well here to say a few words on this silk armour, as it was frequently mentioned and we will come across it again. Grose in his *Military Antiquities* has a drawing of a suit he had seen at Mr. Cosway's and which he believes to have been armour of this kind. He describes it as "being

FIG. 93. Train of Artillery, 1688.

strongly quilted and stuffed besides which it seems strengthened either with jacked leather or thin iron plates, sewed on in the nature of a brigandine. The headpiece has also an iron cap between the outside and the lining. The whole is covered by cinnamon coloured silk" (Figs. 89 and 98). This same colour is mentioned elsewhere in writing of this kind of defensive armour.

Armour is repeatedly mentioned as being issued by the Board of Ordnance to officers of the train. It consisted of breast and back plates and pots with sometimes an elbow gauntlet. Somewhat similar armour consisting of helmet, back and breast plates continued to be issued to the French Engineer Corps for work in the trenches during a siege up to the Second Empire.

Whereas red is always given as the colour of the uniform of the Artillery during this period we have an exception in the train sent with the army to Ireland in 1688, which was dressed in blue and orange, probably in compliment to William III. The clothing of the Pioneers consisted of blue coats lined orange, orange coloured waistcoats, blue breeches, stockings and caps embroidered with a shovel in the front. There were also suits for 2 Sergeants (Fig. 93), 2 Corporals and a Drummer, besides 200 drivers and fourteen suits for the Master Smith and his assistants. The arms for the Gunners and Matrosses were 3 halberds, 80 short pikes, 30 hangers with belts, 146 long carbines strapt, 140 cartouche boxes, 50 pairs of pistols and 18 sets of bits, bridles and troop saddles.

In 1689 the Gunners, Matrosses and tradesmen for the train were to have "blue coats lined orange bayes (baize) with brass buttons and hats with orange silk galoone. The carter's coats to be grey lined orange" (Fig. 93).

It may be as well to mention here the source of the statement often made that gunners wore a blue uniform faced with red as far back as 1642, in fact several drawings reconstructed from this data have already been published. The starting point of all this is the portrait of William Eldred, some time Master Gunner of Dover Castle. This forms the frontispiece of an exceedingly rare book of which he is the author entitled *Ye Gunners Glasse*, published in 1642. This portrait has been coloured at a much later date, probably by some gunner with more *esprit de corps* than knowledge of dress. On carefully examining this engraving we found that it is typical of many other similar portraits of the time, as Eldred is wearing a tight leather jerkin fastened in the customary way with leather lacing; round his neck he has a small fall-down linen collar. This has been coloured as follows: the jerkin as a blue single-breasted coat or jacket, the lacing yellow and in the form of that adopted in the Army in 1799, and the linen collar and cuffs are red edged with yellow, the whole forming the appearance of the uniform coat worn about the above date, but with the turn-down collar of 1770.

For the train in Flanders 1695–97 we come back to red again, the Pioneers being dressed in red coats lined blue, red cloth caps faced with blue, embroidered with Lord Romney's coat of arms and "trophies of Pioneers," white stockings, grey breeches, and shoes.

FIG. 94. A galloper gun and munition cart, 1705.

The Gunners crimson coats lined and faced blue, flap pockets, the blue cuffs edged with gold lace, brass buttons, gold lace loops for the button-holes, blue cloth waistcoats with sleeves and blue Padua cuffs, flap pockets and brass buttons with silk buttonholes; blue stockings, black hats edged with gold and hat bands, gauntlet gloves and shoes.

The Drummers crimson coats lined blue, blue cuffs, laced "everywhere" with gold colour and blue silk lace, brass buttons and silk buttonholes. Hats, waistcoats, breeches, stockings and shoes as for the Gunners.

Sergeants crimson coats lined blue with blue cuffs with a narrow gold galloon edging to the cuffs and pocket flaps and down the front of coat, gold laced buttonholes and buttons, black hats with gold scalloped lace edging and band. The rest as for the Gunners.

Fig. 95. A mortar, 1699.

The Corporal had a similar dress except silver lace in lieu of gold.

In October, 1696. For the train of Artillery in Flanders red coats lined blue and cloth capes (i.e. collars), sleeves and capes edged with gold coloured galloon and loops of same, red cloth waistcoats with brass buttons and red breeches.

1697. For the Matrosses red coats lined and faced blue, blue waistcoats with brass buttons, blue breeches, blue stockings to "rowle." Tann'd leather gloves with tops lined.

For the Gunners crimson coats lined blue, blue cuffs bound with gold binding, gilt buttons and buttonholes of red silk and looped with gold; blue waistcoats with blue sleeves and sleeve bands (wrist bands or cuffs), blue silk buttonholes and brass buttons, blue stockings to "rowle," gold laced hats, gloves with tops.

Sergeants crimson coats lined blue, blue cuffs "laced with 3 gold laces down before and 1 round each open and 1 round each flapps and cuffs, gold topt buttons, red silk holes loopt with gold," hats with broad gold edging. The rest as for Gunners, Corporals the same as Sergeants except silver lace instead of gold.

Drummers crimson coats lined blue, blue cuffs; laced with a broad gold coloured lace and blue silk all over, and bound on all edges with a small silk edging; brass buttons and silk holes; hats edged with gold, rest as for Gunners.

[169]

N

The description of the dress of the Kettle Drummer is so complicated and confused as to be well-nigh incomprehensible, but is intended to mean a crimson coat lined blue with blue cuffs. It is heavily laced with broad gold and silver orris as follows: Two bands of lace down the front with button-hole loops between, down all seams of sleeves, shoulders, back, the skirt openings and round the bottom. There is a lace at the back of the waist and two round the edges of the cuffs. The sleeves have six laces running round horizontally. Besides all this "ten laces on the body and round each side" are mentioned, and a narrow lace between the broad. This may possibly mean a narrow silver lace between the two gold ones, His Majesty's crown and cypher embroidered on the chest and back. The whole is obviously an attempt to describe a coat heavily laced like those worn to-day by the Trumpeters of the Household Cavalry on State occasions, having gold laced buttonhole loops between two bands of the same down the front. The skirts and pocket flaps are laced and the cuffs have three bands of the same. Hats bound silver and gold lace; breeches, stockings, shoes and gloves as for the Gunners, surtout coat, crimson lined blue with blue cuffs, red cloth buttons topt with gold and red silk buttonholes loopt with gold." Belt of crimson cloth laced all over with the same lace as on the coat.

The Kettledrum Driver, crimson coat laced two gold laces down the front and all openings, edges, seams and sleeves with blue velvet between the laces. Waistcoat blue having two gold laces on each side down the front and four on each cuff, brass buttons and silk buttonholes, hat with silver lace as the Corporals, breeches, shoes, stockings and gloves as for the Gunners. Surtout as for Kettle Drummer.

1697. The Pioneers are dressed as previously described, with caps still embroidered with Lord Romney's arms, the only difference being that grey breeches are mentioned.

The Trains formed for William III's campaigns on the Continent had assumed considerable proportions, with a varying strength for the different detachments, the Engineer officers being from 6 to 12 in number, a controller and his clerks and a Captain Lieutenant, a Battery master and his assistant, an adjutant, a quartermaster, a chaplain, a Paymaster and assistant, an auditor, a master surgeon and assistant, a Provost Marshall and assistant, the Kettle Drummer and his driver. The Mortar Detachment under the

FIG. 96. Pontoons and Wagons. 1700–1714.

command of a Petardier, 1 to 4 fire masters, 19 fireworkers and 4 to 30 Bombardiers. The artillery officered by a Captain-Lieutenant, 6 or 8 gentlemen of the ordnance, a master gunner, his two mates, 2 corporals, 40 to 92 gunners and 80 or 92 matrosses. The Company of Bridgement or Pontooniers under a Captain of the Boats, his assistant or Lieutenant, 2 corporals and 30 to 40 privates, a detachment of Miners under a sergeant, a Company of Pioneers under N.C.O.S., the various artificers and their mates, the Master carpenter, for instance, having two mates and 17 carpenters.

The Store and Transport were managed by two Commissaries of Stores, two clerks, 8 to 18 conductors of Stores, 2 conductors of woolpacks, a purveyor and his assistant, a waggon-master and mate, 4 conductors of horses, a commissary of draught horses and his mate and 70 drivers, 600 horses for the guns and the boats (of which there were 40). 600 horses with 200 waggons for the transport of stores, ammunition, entrenching tools, tents, etc.

The guns for the Train which served at Steinkirk and Landen consisted of 8 demi-culverins of 9 lbs., 10 sakers about 6 Prs. 20 –3 Prs. 4–8 inch howitzers and 2 small petards, all brass. Another consisted of 14–24 Prs. 16–18 Prs. 8 13 inch howitzers, 6 brass petards, 12 10-inch mortars and 20,000 grenades. These Trains were what one might compare to-day as an amalgamation of Royal Artillery, Royal Engineers, Royal Army Ordnance Corps and the horse transport of the Royal Army Service Corps.

The Engineer officers formed an integral part of the Artillery Train, and as such seemed to have served in the dual capacity of Engineer and Artillery-man, the Train itself, as often as not, being commanded by the Chief Engineer.

The Engineers had existed in the previous century under the various titles

FIG. 97. Pack mules and baggage waggons, 1706.

of Trench Masters, Captains of Pioneers, and field works. Those selected for fortress work were called surveyors. Charles I was one of the first Sovereigns to strengthen and improve this branch of the service by securing the best men, some English, some foreign, the latter being mostly Dutch. Three Engineer officers appear to have been permanently attached to the Ordnance service. At the Restoration this staff of three officers was renewed. This establishment was quite insufficient for the necessities of the service, and in 1669 a Warrant was issued for two cadets to be sent abroad to visit foreign fortresses and gain experience and training by taking part in sieges and campaigns. The title of Cadet was shortly changed to Engineer.

At times when extra Engineers were required either for some special work at home or in the colonies or for any expedition these were taken into pay and when their duties terminated they were either discharged or placed on half pay, so as to be available again if required. There was also an Irish Ordnance, which was an entirely separate department on its own. In 1669 this had three Engineers serving on it, one of whom was called the Engineer and Overseer of fortifications. Scotland also had its own separate Ordnance Board.

About 1683 the Engineer officers of the Ordnance Board were made responsible for the construction and maintenance of the military work and fortresses of the country.

Two ordinary Engineers were attached to the Ordnance "to be bred up in the art and knowledge of fortifications."

In 1698 a Train of reduced strength was permanently maintained during the Peace.

ARTILLERY

In 1702 six Engineer officers were attached to a Train sent to Gibraltar in addition to the artillery branch and a number of artificers and their mates were sent out. These were to be in charge of a large body of men raised, or rather hired, locally, to carry out work on the fortifications.

Engineers had no distinct military rank, and in consequence disputse

FIG. 98. Engineer Officers and Pioneers, *c.* 1700.

arose over the distribution of prize money. This was finally settled by Royal Authority Dec. 16th, 1692, which decreed that Engineers were to receive prize money at the rate of 15 shares each.

Engineer officers also served on the Staff, as Lt.-Colonel Richards and Captain John Armstrong, who acted as Quartermaster-General.

As regards the dress of the Engineer and Artillery officers, it seems probable that there was no difference between the two branches in view of the fact that they were considered to be officers of one and the same Corps, the Ordnance.

Colonel Wolfgang Romer, an Engineer of the Ordnance, is represented in his portrait wearing a plain blue coat lined red with red cuffs; under this he has a steel cuirass (Fig. 98).

An account dated March 22nd, 1707 mentions, besides other items, "blew cloath for ye officers cloathes." Colonel James Pendlebury, Master

FIG. 99. Officer of Artillery, c. 1709.

gunner 1709 (Fig. 99), in his portrait wears a scarlet coat lined blue with blue cuffs, which as well as the waist-coat is richly embroidered with gold. He wears a cuirass and his waist is encircled with a gold fringed crimson sash. Another portrait of an officer of the Ordnance depicts a plain red coat and cuffs, a cuirass and buff waistcoat. From this it appears that Ordnance officers wore red coats or blue faced with red similar to those shown in the groups of Staff officers.

The detachments or companies of Miners, Pontooniers and Pioneers, which formed part of the Trains in garrisons or in the field from the fact that they were uniformed and armed, are not to be confused with the bodies of labourers hired locally for some specific work, but may be considered, as far as the rank and file is concerned, as the predecessors of the Engineer companies. As early as the occupation of Tangier a military company of Miners was formed under the command of Captain A. Basset and consisted of 3 N.C.O.'s and 41 Miners.

Under the supervision and inspiration of Marlborough the trains of Artillery, which accompanied his army on the Continent, were to lay the foundation of the proud record of service which has been carried on by their successors to the present day. Eye-witnesses are unanimous in their praise of the efficiency, devotion and untiring energy of the officers and men both in working their guns and in getting their cumbersome pieces over the execrable roads in time to take their share in gaining the Duke's victories.

During the campaign of 1702 the fire of the artillery is described as having been carried out with "as much order, dispatch and success as ever before was seen." Hare, His Grace's Secretary, writes in his *Journal* of the gunners having surmounted difficulties of getting up our heavy cannon, which the enemy flattered themselves was impossible at Blenheim. Marlborough himself saw to the placing of the guns, and the concentration of the great battery at Malplaquet was also due to his grasp of artillery fire. An Engineer officer, Colonel Blood, as Chief of the Ordnance Train, directed the movements of the artillery at Blenheim and for his services was promoted Brigadier-General. The guns were 3 Prs., 6 Prs., 9 to 11 Prs., 18 Prs. and 36 Prs., and even 60 Prs. During the later half of the seventeenth century the 3 Prs. were attached in pairs to battalions of Foot; the heavier guns would seemingly form the batteries. Atkinson in his *Marlborough and The Rise of the British Army* says that guns larger than 24 Prs. were seldom used in the field, even in sieges. The ammunition was carried in wagons. These were originally ordinary farm wagons, but from engravings, etc., a military vehicle with a roof-shaped covering now seems to have come into use. Some of these are shown with two wheels and others four. Mortars, by this time, were also mounted on field carriages, and were supplied to Peterborough for his campaign in Spain, together with "sets of men harness," no doubt in view of dragging guns over difficult country (Fig. 100).

Previously the powder was placed in the gun with a long scoop-shaped ladle, and it was considered a "foul Fault" on the part of the gunner in so doing to withdraw even the smallest quantity of power or even spill a few grains on the ground. The gunner, himself, was advised "to set forth himself with as comely a posture and grace as he can, for agility and comely carriage, in handling the ladle and sponge, doth give great content to standers by."

FIG. 100. Mortar on Field Carriage, *c.* 1709.

Instead of this, by the end of the seventeenth century, the charge was previously made up in bags of vellum, paper or canvas. The ammunition is also shown being brought to guns in wheelbarrows from the wagons.

A bill to Jane Hill, July 3rd, 1713 gives some curious details, viz: "For painting 24 Rocket chests finished in white edged with black, each 15/-.

"24 cyphers and crown painted in proper colours upon the Rocket chests, 15/- each.

"Painting 4 Balloons finished white and striped with black at 2/6 each.

"Painting in proper colours 8 union arms on 4 flags upon the Balloons.

"Painting 12 flag staves finished white the balls yellow 4/- each.

"Rockets painted red and blue."

The Rockets were used for signals. The balloons are puzzling and there seems to be no record of them at Woolwich. The Oxford Dictionary, however, gives the following description: "A ball of pasteboard stuffed with combustible matter, which when fired from a mortar mounts to a considerable height in the air and then bursts, with bright sparks of fire resembling stars." Even so, it does not seem clear what was their actual use or why so much money should have been spent on their decoration.

FIG. 101. Transport waggon, Marlborough's campaigns.

The models of the different vehicles used by Marlborough's Train show the transport wagon, which is simply the farm type of the period, but was evidently maintained as the service model for some considerable time afterwards, as we shall come across it again.

ARTILLERY

A small-sized mortar was used for trench work with the infantry, much in the same way as in the Great War. These were called Cohorns after the famous Dutch Engineer officer of William III, who is said to have invented them.

The field forge is evidently much in advance of that used

FIG. 102. Field Forge, Marlborough's Train of Artillery.

on the Continent, as French paintings show one mounted on a tripod and placed in a waggon for transport (Fig. 102).

During the siege of Tournay in 1709 a realistic description is given in *The Daily Courant* August 10th of the underground fighting with mine and counter-mine. "Our miners and the enemy very often meet each other, when they have sharp combats, till one side gives way, we have got into three or four of the enemys great Galleries, which are thirty or forty feet underground and lead to several of their chambers, and in these we fight in armour by lanthorn and candle, they disputing every inch of the gallery with us to hinder our finding out their great mines. Yesternight we found one which was placed just under our bomb batteries, in which were 18 cwt of powder besides many bombs, and if we had not been so lucky as to find it, in a very few hours our batteries and some hundreds of men had taken a flight into the air."

In the Victoria and Albert Museum is a cap made entirely of red material embroidered with white, the little flap being worked with an interlaced cypher, which may have been that of the Captain. There is no means of stating that the cap is English, but it, at any rate, agrees in colour and shape with those caps shown in the borders of trophies on the Blenheim tapestries. As the turn-up at the back of the cap has a pair of crossed pickaxes it is possible that it is the cap worn by a Miner detachment rather than a Pioneer (Fig. 103).

In 1702 the dress of the Kettle Drummer was still as before except that the colour of the richly laced coat and surtout was scarlet instead of crimson. The Kettle Drum driver also had a scarlet coat laced with gold and lined with blue, blue waistcoat and breeches, plain hat and worsted stockings. The Drummers of the Artillery companies were the same as the Kettle Drum driver, but had in addition belts laced as their coats and fitted with swivels.

"The Drum banners each with Her Majesty's arms richly embroidered on

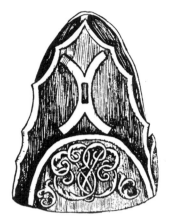

FIG. 103. Pioneer or Miner's cap.

the finest Genoa damask of proper colours with fringes and tassels and cases of good oyle cloth."

1702. For the Sergeants, large surtout coats of crimson cloth lined blue shalloon and brass buttons and pockets.

For Corporals, Gunners and Pontoonmen, large surtout coats of red lined blue with brass buttons and pockets.

1703. The arms sent to Portugal for the artillery, Bombardiers, Gunners, and Miners: hangers with brass hilts; snaphances with long bayonet(te)s, Red coats lined blue, blue waistcoats.

London Gazette April 22nd, 1708—Matrosses deserted from Her Majesty's Train of artillery at Blackheath, one wears a red turned coat, lined with black, black buttons and buttonholes, black waistcoat and red breeches. This was possibly mourning dress.

From the lists of materials sent to the Train in Spain and Port Mahon in 1710 we find that the Bombardiers and Artificers wore scarlet coats lined blue, and the Gunners, Matrosses, etc., red, lined blue.

Another list for the Train in Flanders: For the Sergeants and Corporals scarlet coats laced gold and blue cloth breeches laced; the Gunners and

ARTILLERY

Pontoon men scarlet coats lined blue and blue breeches. The Matrosses and Pyoneers red coats and blue breeches.

In 1712 the Artillery in Spain, the Sergeants and Corporals wore gold laced hats and the company yellow. Blue breeches and waistcoats as before.

FIG. 104. Artillery, c. 1708.

GENERAL OFFICERS

THERE seem to have been no rules regarding the dress of general officers, nor can one find any distinction of rank.

In the earlier pictures they are occasionally shown wearing coats entirely covered with a gold embroidered pattern. James II in one portrait wears a

FIG. 105. James II.

coat with very wide bands of gold lace following the lines of the seams and the spaces between heavily embroidered. In other cases Generals are pictured in buff coats, worked with gold thread, generally in circles round the sleeves, thus continuing the fashion in vogue in the reign of Charles I. A sash of crimson or crimson and gold net was worn round the waist or over the shoulder according to the fashion of the moment. Loops of ribbons on the shoulders are sometimes shown and Colonel Clifford Walton says the

FIG. 106. Saddle and holster caps of the Duke of Monmouth.

aiguillette was worn in the latter part of the seventeenth century as indicating the rank of a General, but this was not usual, as only one instance of it appears to be known.

The cuirass is often shown worn under the coat and over the waistcoat. The waistcoat is often of buff and sometimes laced round the edges and pocket flaps with gold lace. It is needless to say that although military portraits of this period, as well as those of a much later date, show the sitter in armour, this was merely a convention of the time and does not mean that it was still in use.

The hat was bound with gold lace and ornamented with a profusion of feathers.

In studying the mural paintings at Marlborough House and the tapestries at Blenheim, besides other paintings of the period, there still seems to be no means of distinguishing the ranks of the different officers of Marlborough's Staff. The Duke, himself, is wearing the Star and Ribbon of the Garter. His Generals are habited in scarlet or blue coats, both of which have red cuffs. These coats are single-breasted, laced along the seams and ornamented down the front with laced or embroidered loops on the buttonholes, some of these loops are finished off at the ends by small tassels. Sometimes the coat is shown lined and edged with fur.

The breeches are generally buff-coloured, but some are of scarlet cloth,

FIG. 107 Details of housings and holster caps of William III.

and in some instances these have a broad gold lace down the outer seam as had already been a fashion in the time of Charles I.

The sash is generally shown worn round the waist, but one or two of the Staff are wearing it over the right shoulder.

The hats are bound with gold lace and often decorated with a loop and button of the same. Others, again, are trimmed with feathers along the inside edges of the brim.

In the Blenheim tapestries one officer is shown with a large hound bounding alongside his horse. This figure is said to represent Cadogan who, it is stated, like Prince Rupert, was accompanied by a favourite hound while campaigning. Cadogan was Quartermaster-General, his duties, however, resembling those of a Chief of Staff.

"For short distances or less important orders, the runners we see in the tapestries with their long brass-headed staves of authority were used." *Churchill's Marlborough*, Vol. II, p. 115.

These Runners are frequently shown in the Blenheim Tapestries.[1]

Stanhope in his portrait is represented wearing a plain blue coat with cuffs of the same colour, a cuirass with three vertical bands of a gold inlaid design and underneath this he wears a buff waistcoat bound with gold lace on the edges and pocket flaps. One curious point in this picture is that he is wearing a small moustache, which is not shown in any other of his portraits. However,

FIG. 108. Details of housings and holster caps of the Duke of Marlborough.

as he has rather an unshaven appearance, this is perhaps to give the effect of his being on active service. The portraits of this period show their sitters as being clean shaven.

A long baton carried in the hand is nearly always shown to indicate the Commander. According to Meyrick and Skelton this emblem of command was of Greek origin, the Lacedemonian scytale being its prototype. They go on to say that it was used for secret correspondence and described it as follows: "The scytale was a plain truncheon and two of the same dimensions being made, one was delivered to the General and the other retained by the Lacedemonian magistrates. When the former had occasion to send home a despatch he took a strip of parchment and twisting it spirally round the staff, wrote across the edges what he wished to communicate. This, when the parchment was unrolled, became unintelligible, nor could it be comprehended until wrapped round the corresponding baton."

The horse furniture, housings and holster caps are nearly always red, embroidered in gold with a wide lace edging and sometimes further enriched

[1] See Fig. 49, p. 50.

with a deep gold fringe. The holster caps are cut in a very rounded shape, falling in deep folds.

A very typical design of the embroidery is rather like an acanthus starting from the rear corner of the saddle cloth and breaking into scrolls covering the whole surface.

FIG. 108A. William III.

MILITIA

TRAIN BANDS, HONOURABLE ARTILLERY COMPANY

1660–1714

THE Militia which was descended from the ancient Saxon Fyrd and the Posse Comitatus of feudal times, was for centuries the main defensive force of the country up to 1660.

In the sixteenth century we read of the Train, or Trained Bands, which are described as being "the hablest men selected from the levies."

Charles II decided to reorganise the country militia and make it more efficient. The old controversial question as to whether the command of this force was in the hands of the Sovereign or Parliament, was settled by various Acts passed during this reign which vested "the sole and supreme command" in the Crown.

Under the reorganization the Train Bands, except those of London, and their auxiliaries were abolished, and the Militia of each county was placed under the immediate command of the Lord Lieutenant, who was empowered to grant commissions to officers "with the power of the King to displace them."

The Militia of the Tower Division, commonly called The Tower Hamlets, was always under the command of the Constable, or Lieutenant, of the Tower.

The Militia at this time consisted of infantry and in many cases troops of Horse as well. The arms of a trooper were "a breast and back plate, a pot, pistol proof, a sword, a case of pistols, the barrels not under 14 inches in length. For the horse, a great saddle or pad, with bars and straps for affixing the holsters, a bit, a bridle, with pectoral and crupper."
For the Foot:

A Musketeer—a musket, the barrel not under three feet in length and the gauge of the bore for 12 bullets to the pound, a collar of bandoliers, and a sword.

The Pikeman was armed with "a pike of ash not under 16 feet in length (head and foot included)" with back and breast plates, head piece, and a sword. From some reference it seems that tassets were also worn occasionally.

At every muster and exercise the Musketeer was to bring with him half a pound of powder, half a pound of bullets, and every Musketeer serving with a matchlock to bring with him three yards of match. Every horseman to bring with him a quarter of a pound of powder and a quarter of a pound of bullets.

FIG. 109. Leading staves.

Although coats of various colours are mentioned the Militia seem to have claimed the right to wear red, as the Governor of Exeter having raised a regiment of Foot in 1662 clad them in red coats. From a reference of a later date the coat only was given out as uniform, but the breeches were whatever the militiaman had of his own.

A document in the British Museum (Stow MS.) gives some interesting details of the Kent Militia in 1668 as follows: "Whereas there was an order made and agreed upon ye 21st of May last, past by the Lord Lieutenant and Deputy Lieutenants of the county of Kent, at the city of Rochester, the General and respective soldiers of ye Militia of the said county should appear in red coats (except the regiment belonging to the Lord Lieutenant, who are to appear in yellow coats, lined black, down to ye knees and according to the usual custom of soldiers) These as theretofore to will and require you to take caire that ye general soldiers of your company be clothed accordingly, and if in case ye any person or persons, of your company doth deny or refuse to be obedient to this order, that you return his name unto me or in my absence, unto any two or more of my Deputy Lieutenants given under our hands this 2 June 1668.

P.S. You are to declare that in lieu of their coats, they are discharged from their defensive arms, which is back, breast, and corselet (in this case would mean tassets)."

In an account of the progress of the Duke of Beaufort as Lord Marcher in 1688 T. Dinely gives short descriptions of several of the Militia corps in Glamorganshire—"a regiment of Foot clothed in purple, lined red, red stockings, broad buff coloured shoulder belts, and girt with white sashes:

1 Troop of Horse under Lord Arthur, 2nd son of Duke of Beaufort, also purple, lined red" (Fig. 110, A).

"*Caernarvon:* 1 Troop of Horse, and 1 regt. of Foot of 3 companies."

"*Caermardon*—1 Troop of Horse with black Standard fringed and tasseled with gold and silver. 1 Regt. of Foot under Sir Rice Williams."

"*Flintshire*—5 companies of Foot: Captain Sir Roger Mostyn, Bart., his company all clothed with red lined with red, broad belts and white sashes, red stockings and new hats, edged and turned up on ye side with buttons, at his own proper charge. A stand of Pikes. Troop of Horse under Sir John Hanmere, Bart."

"*Brecknock.* His Grace took a view of the militia in a meadow near the town, a Troop with a Captain, Lieutenant, Cornet and Quartermaster and five companies with green colours. The regt is commanded by a Colonel, Captains, Lieutenants, and Ensigns. The foot were clad in new hats, blue cassocks, white sashes edged with blue worsted fringe, broad buff coloured shoulder belts, and red yarn stockings.

"The Horse appeared well mounted with buff coats, carbines, pistols, back, breast and potts, bridles and collars, huisses (housings) with their cloaks strapp'd behind them."

Anglesey (Merionethshire). "Troop of Horse commanded by Capt. Bulkeley Esq. 4 companies of foot, Beaumarice company having a red colour with a red cross in a canton and the other three companies blue colours" (Fig. 110, B).

"*Merionethshire*, at Rulas, 1 small Troop of Horse. Standard with *Non Palma sine Pulvere* in gold. 2 companies of Foot."

"*Montgomeryshire.* 4 companies of Foot with white colour and 1 Troop of Horse, standard of damask carrieth a dexter arm, arm'd proper, holding a heart gules and in an escrowle this wrote *Pro Rege* with tazzels of gold silk and silver."

"*Pembrokeshire.* A Troop of Horse under a standard of flowered damask, with gold and silk fringe and tazzels carrying 'For God and the King.' 1 reg. of Foot, all of fire-locks, 8 companies." (Fig. 110, C).

"*Radnorshire.* Caermarion, Cardiganshire, Denbighshire are all mentioned as being composed of a Troop of Horse and companies of Foot, but no description of their dress.

The Duke of Beaufort in his progress was accompanied "by four Trumpeters in very rich coats having his cypher in gold, under a ducal crown, on the backs and breasts; and each with a silver trumpet, with gold and silver strings and tazzels, crimson flower'd damask banners, embroidered with ye coat of arms of the Duke of Beaufort, viz: Sovereign of France and England, quarterly in bordure gorbonated pearl and sapphire, all within a garter with his Grace's motto in a compartment *Mutare Vel Timere Sperno.*"

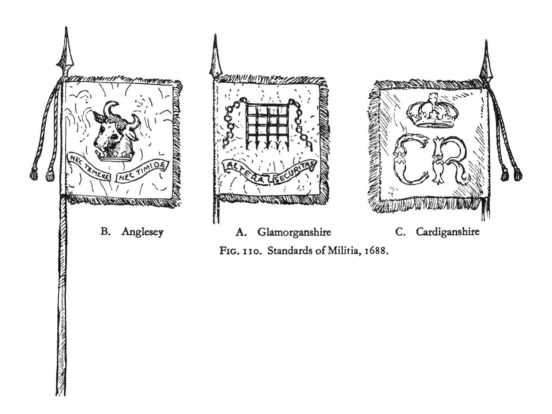

B. Anglesey   A. Glamorganshire   C. Cardiganshire

FIG. 110. Standards of Militia, 1688.

Gloucester Militia "All in their buff coats." *London Gazette* July 23rd–26th, 1666.

The St. Helena records 1683–85 mention that the Militia of the island wore red coats.

Surrey Musters, Loseley MSS. XXXV. 1684 17 May To the High Constables of the Hundred of Blackheath . . . to finde foote Souldiers and Arms in the Company of Captaine Austen, that they send in their Souldiers, with

FIG. 111. City Train Bands 1586.

their Arms compleatly Fixed and Furnished and Red Coates, to be and appeare att Guldeford, . . .

The Suffolk Militia regiments in 1697 according to Clifford Walton were dressed in red, white, blue and yellow uniforms, and the officers having crimson sashes.

"The Militia regiment of Middlesex is to be forthwith new clothed in a red coat, faced with grey cloth, and a hat edged with gold colour galoon, and a bayonet fix'd to the muskets, and in room of pikes, to have new muskets."—*Post Boy*, July 10th, 1712.

The Train Bands of London were recruited only from the citizens and householders and not from the prentices, as has often been stated, as these last not having the necessary qualifications, were only allowed to join the auxiliary formations.

A representation of the funeral procession of Sir Philip Sidney shows men of the Train Bands, with matchlocks reversed, and the ensign and pikes at the trail, which in this case means actually trailing the pike or ensign point downwards on the ground (Fig. 111).

The troops shown in an engraving of the procession of Queen Henrietta Maria through Cheapside, are said to be the London Train Bands, which were on duty lining the streets for the occasion. They are dressed in the usual costume of the time of short jackets and full breeches.

The regiments were called the Red, Blue, Orange, Green, White, and Yellow, but this applied to their colours and not to their coats.

FIG. 112. City Train Bands, 1688.

During the Civil War the officers wore red coats laced with silver, one letter of the time mentioning that this had become tarnished with exposure. When the Parliament forces were put into red coats, the Train Bands had them also, it being even possible that they were already so dressed before this. The Tower Guards formed half-way through the Civil War as a garrison for the Tower, were part of the Train Bands.

The Train Bands fought well at the battles of Newbury and Colchester, and also served in Ireland towards the end of the War.

At the Restoration the London Train Bands had the reputation of being the most efficient. A contemporary and crude cartoon of the arrest of Judge Jeffreys, who was escorted by men of the Train Bands, shows two men of this force. They are wearing the cassocks or long coats, full breeches and wide-brimmed felt hats of the period (Fig. 112).

In 1697 the Musketeers wore buff coats, red feathers in their hats, and white stockings.

In 1701 the officers were dressed in blue coats, gilt gorgets, beaver hats with feathers, scarlet stockings and sashes. Marshals in buff coats.

The rank and file, felt hats, buff coats, or frocks, and helmets.

1710, caps, pouches and slings for Grenadiers.

The officers were mostly drawn from that curious and ancient organization which, under varying titles as the "Artillery Yard," "Artillery Garden," etc., finally became the Honourable Artillery Company. Its origin is lost in antiquity, but the first known date of its existence is 1537, when Henry VIII granted a charter to the "Guylde of St. George," a fraternity "to be overseers of the science of artillery, that is to witt, long bowes, cross bowes, and hand gonnes . . . for the better encrease of the defence of our realme."

Stow in his Chronicles says that in 1598 "the London cityzen who had had experience, both at home and abroad, voluntarily enrolled themselves in the Company, and trained up others, for the wars, so that in two years there were about 300 merchants and others of like quality, capable of training common soldiers, the management of their pieces, pikes and halberts, to march counter march and ring."

During the alarm caused by the Spanish Armada the City Train Bands encamped at Tilbury, were largely officered by members of the Company. This was again the case when the Train Bands were mustered during the Civil War, and it was no doubt due to the training of these officers that these troops put up such a stout resistance at the Battle of Newbury.

From all this it is clear that the Company was an early example of an Officers' Training Corps.

So useful did the Company prove itself, that others on similar lines were started in different parts of London and the provinces. The engraving of Henry Prince of Wales, son of James I, performing the pike drill, is said to represent a view of the Artillery Yard of Westminster in the background.

The figures taken from the supporters of the early seventeenth century armorial bearings of the Company, seem to have been traditionally coloured, with buff and red coats and red breeches. They represent an officer of Pikes and one of Musketeers, and they are both shown booted and spurred, no doubt to emphasise the fact that they are officers.

At Charles II's entry into London in 1660 the officers of the Company are described as wearing buff coats with sleeves of cloth of silver and green scarves.

From repeated references during the years 1674, 1678, 1683, 1684, 1694 and 1702, all of which give the same details of dress, it is clear that the uniform of the Company was a buff coat and a metal head-piece with red plumes.

In 1674, for instance, the Musketeers are ordered "to provide themselves with bright head-pieces and plumes of red feathers, it having been the ancient and constant custom for the Musketeers to march so accoutred." In another place it says that "many of the Musketeers' head-pieces were of massive silver, and that most of the Pike men as well as officers, wore very rich embroidered belts."

The Corps had drums and fifes and in 1686 three hautboys, or hautbois, were added.

In 1693 a leading staff with a finely decorated head was presented to the Company. This staff is still preserved by the Corps and is shown held in the mailed hand which is the crest forming part of the Company's coat-of-arms (Fig. 109).

A surgeon was first posted to the Company in 1663 and was ordered to be supplied with a scarf. This scarf is again mentioned in 1727, so it appears

FIG. 113. Grenadier of the Honourable Artillery Company, "Sling your Fire lock."

FIG. 114. Grenadier Cap of the Honourable Artillery Company.

to have been regarded as an emblem or badge of the profession. In view of the word scarf and not sash being used, one is tempted to imagine that it may have been some kind of belt made of cloth in which the surgeon carried his instruments, dressings, etc.

In 1667 Pioneers with their implements are already mentioned as marching at the head of the Corps, and in 1670 we read that a train of artillery formed part of the Company, with its gunners, matrosses and escort of firelocks. This train in 1674 was composed of six guns and two waggons and was attended by 24 Marshals in buff coats, armed with blunderbusses.

A number of the Corps were trained in 1686 in the duties of Grenadiers and wore in addition to their buff coats, caps of crimson velvet lined with rich fur. In 1711 these Grenadiers were replaced by Fuziliers, but in 1714 it was decided to re-establish the Grenadiers and caps, pouches, slings for fuzees for 2 Lieutenants, 2 Flankers and 24 Grenadiers were purchased besides caps and coats for two Drummers (Fig. 114).

Two caps of the time of Queen Anne exist; one at the Corps' headquarters and another at the Victoria and Albert Museum. They are entirely of crimson velvet with the portcullis, crown, and Queen Anne's cypher on the little flap, in silver. The back has a grenade worked in the same material. A coat-of-arms of this date has a Grenadier and musketeer of the Corps introduced as supporters. They are dressed in the uniform of the period, the Grenadier's cap having a portcullis on the front, and the pouches of both men are decorated with the same device (Figs. 113 and 115).

FIG. 115. Musketeer of the Honourable Artillery Company.

The colours of the London Train Bands are all shown in Harl. MS. 986 B.M. They exemplify the rules explained by Captain Venn, the Colonel's a plain red, yellow, etc., according to the colour of the regiment; the Lt.-Colonel's the same but with a red cross on white in the upper canton; the Major's the same with a pile wavy, lozenge or star placed at the lower corner of the canton; the 2nd Captain two, and so on.

The Red Regiment. Red colours. Major's and Company Captains' indicated by one or more piles wavy issuing from the lower corner of the canton.

The White Regiment. White ensigns. Major's and Company devices, 1–5, red diamonds.

The Yellow Regiment. Yellow ensigns with black stars arranged as above up to the 4th Captain; the 5th as per Fig.

The Blue Regiment. Blue, as the Yellow Regiment, but with white balls or roundels.

The Green Regiment. Green with white caltraps arranged diagonally.

The Orange Regiment. Orange with white trefoils arranged as per Fig.

Westminster Liberty. Red ensigns, white six-pointed stars arranged diagonally.

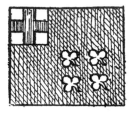
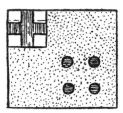

Captain's colour, 4th Captain's, 3rd Captain's, Colonel's,
The Orange Regt. Southwark Regt. Tower Hamlets.

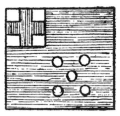

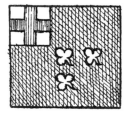

Captain's colour, Captain's colour, Captain's colour, 3rd Captain's,
The Red Regt. The Blue Regt. The Green Regt. The Orange Regt.

FIG. 116. Colours of the Train Bands.

Southwark Regiment. Yellow ensigns, the Major's in this case has the pile wavy. First and third Captains' by blue roundels arranged diagonally. The 4th, 5th and 6th as per sketch.

The Tower Hamlets are more elaborate, being of red and having the motto JEHOVA PROVIDE BIT within white or silver branches and having sprigs of white leaves in the corners, the Major's and Company Captains' ensigns being distinguished by white roundels placed in a row along the top of the ensign.

The Auxiliaries followed much the same principles as the Train Bands, except that most used one to five piles wavy, as already described, to indicate the Major and Company Captains, the green, white, yellow, blue Auxiliaries having them of gold, red, blue and gold respectively.

The Red and Orange Auxiliaries used white roundels in a diagonal row, the Orange, however, having a pile wavy for the Major's ensign.

SCOTS MILITIA

In Scotland, the term "Defensible Persons" and later "Fensible Persons" was used in reference to the men who formed the local levies, but by the beginning of the seventeenth century the word "Militia" began to be applied when speaking of those forces, which in England were called the "Train Bands". The expression Train Bands was not current in Scotland, one exception being the City Force of Edinburgh which, like that of London, was recruited from the citizens of the town.

At the Restoration the establishment of a National Militia was authorized by an Act passed September 23rd, 1663. The Force was to consist of 2,000 Horse and 20,000 Foot.

The Crown appointed the Captains of Horse and the Colonels and Lt.-Colonels of Foot, who in their turn selected their Majors. The remaining officers were appointed by the commissioners of Militia, in whose hands the control of the force rested. The commissions of the officers thus selected were issued by the King. Officers commanding units were to be mounted, except in the case of Highland Companies.

The Companies of Foot were to be of a minimum strength of 78 men, and if the foot of any shire was over 1,100, it was to be divided into two regiments. In the case of the "Horse", if a troop was above 80 men, it was to be formed into two troops.

The Militia was to be mustered for training four times a year, and the liability to serve was restricted outside Scotland to England and Ireland.

The equipment was furnished at the expense of the different counties, and every effort was made to ensure uniformity.

The Infantry consisted of one-third Pike-men armed with 15-foot pikes and swords, the remainder being Musketiers, armed with match locks, bandoliers and swords.

A large proportion of the muskets were imported from Holland. To ensure that they were only used in the service of the Crown, match-locks only were issued; as there being only a small quantity of match in the Kingdom, except that which was stored in the Royal Magazine.

FIG. 117. Standard of John Lord Murray's Militia Troop of Horse.

Half a pound of powder, and 2 lbs. of match were issued yearly to each Musketier, and then only when on duty.

The prohibition of flint locks in one case at least produced a strong protest, as it was pointed out that the Highlanders were unused to handling any other kind of musket.

The Horse were armed with swords and pistols, and a roster kept of the horses, with their colours and markings, and horse inspections held four times a year, by a troop officer and a commissioner of Militia.

No records of dress have come to light, although it is considered fairly certain that blue coats were worn by some regiments. This is supported in an old ballad of the period, which describes the Lowland Militia as being dressed in blue coats.

It is highly probable, however, that many units wore uniforms of hodden grey cloth, like the regular army.

Drums, Colours, Standards and Trumpets were provided by the heritors (landed proprietors) of the shires. Infantry colours were to be as follows: The Colonel's to be "plain white, ornamented with what arms or motto he may choose." The remaining colours to be those of Scotland, with the name of the shire in large letters, and distinguished by billets, crescents, stars or numerals, as the Colonel shall think fit. The Standards of Horse were to be plain except the name placed upon them. In the case of the Troop being raised in several shires, these were all to have their names put upon the Standard." The colour of the Standards was left to the choice of the Troop Captain and the shire in which it was raised.

In 1678, the Militia was reduced to 500 Horse and 5,000 Foot, and in 1685 the annual trainings were abolished, except in cases of emergency.

The Force saw service in the various campaigns against the Covenanters.

After the Union we hear little of the Scots Militia, although various attempts were made to revive it; these, however, failed partly from the fear of Jacobite activities, but also from the opposition of some of the Scottish nobles themselves, who feared that the passing of the Militia Act might provide the excuse of having their horses and arms commandeered by powerful and hostile neighbours.

During the years following the accession of George I the Militia remained in a somewhat moribund state for obvious reasons. Though some militia and volunteer units, including a corps of volunteer horse, were formed in the Risings of 1715 and 1717.

In the "'45" Rising again a certain number of Independent corps and volunteers were formed. Such as the Glasgow regiment of volunteers, the Argyllshire militia, the Volunteers and Train Bands of Edinburgh, etc. The last two mentioned corps surrendered the capital to Prince Charles Edward without firing a shot.

The Campbell or Argyll Highland Militia took a prominent part in the battle of Culloden, and by breaking down a park wall on the Jacobite flank

FIG. 118. Officer of Sutherland's Fencibles, c. 1760.

and permitting the cavalry to attack from that direction, contributed in no small degree to the successful result of the action.

The Argyll Militia would have been wearing Highland dress and arms, and possibly the red jacket; like the other Scottish troops on the government side, they would have been wearing the black cockade and red cross in their bonnets. As to the other militia and volunteer units, their dress can only be surmised as being the red or blue coat, which last colour had been worn previously, and again at a later date.

During the Seven Years War, various bills were introduced to raise the Scots Militia, on the same footing as that in England, but in each case they were defeated.

In 1759, however, two Fencible Regiments were raised in the Highlands. These, strictly speaking, were units of the Regular Army raised for the period of the war and service in their own country only. They endured from 1759 to 1763. Alan Ramsay's portrait of the Earl of Sutherland as Colonel of the Sutherland Fencibles shows the uniform worn by the officers, viz., a scarlet jacket and waistcoat, yellow facings, silver lace buttonholes and buttons. Plain blue bonnet with tuft of black feathers, belted plaid of

"Government" tartan, hose of the usual red and white with a black edging to the red. Garters of scarlet with two yellow lines. Silver or steel cut buckles to the shoes, basket hilted broad-sword, and silver-mounted dirk. Badger or wildcat skin sporran with knotted leather cords or tassels. A portrait of Mackay of Strathy, who was a Captain in this Corps, said to have been painted by Zoffany, agrees with the above details, with the addition of a black leather shoulder-belt having a silver buckle, slide, and heart-shaped tip. The other regiment raised was the Argyll Fencibles, which wore a similar uniform and facings, with belted plaid of the same tartan.

JERSEY MILITIA

1660–1714

THE Militia of Jersey originated in 1542, when the Parish Committees were instituted to organise the defences of the Island.

Each Parish raised its own self-contained Train Band known as a Company, the men composing it being termed "companions". The word Militia was not used at this time.

Their first active service was in 1549, when a French fleet, which had been blockading the Islands, was driven off by an inferior squadron under Captain William Wynter. The French in their retreat landed a raiding party at Boulay Bay and were repulsed by the companies of the Islands' Train Bands.

Between 1542 and 1600 the States passed over thirty Acts dealing with the military concerns of the Island. On the Constables fell many onerous responsibilities, viz., the collection of the necessary funds from the none too willing Parishioners, of seeing that the Companions attended parades or turned out for the necessary day and night guards on the coast line; collecting the fatigue parties required for work on the fortifications; see that the free issue of beer, cider and bread was correct and up to standard, and finally be responsible for the care of fire-arms and munitions.

The religious wars of the Continent with their consequent alarms gave the necessary fillip to keeping the companies on the alert and in training. Parades and reviews were frequent and good marksmanship was encouraged. At one review on September 17th, 1585, two silver cups were offered for target practice.

On one occasion, in 1594, 2,700 equipped men were on parade. They are described as strong, active fellows, fairly well armed and as well trained as the usual Train Bands in England.

In 1602 a modification of the self-contained company system took place, in which can be detected the origin of the old Militia regiments.

On the alarm caused by the approach of a Spanish squadron the Parish companies were ordered to assemble, as was customary, at their respective Parish Churches and were grouped in pairs, as follows: St. Helen and St. Lawrence; St. Saviour and St. Martin; St. Clement and Grouville; Trinity and St. John; St. Ouen and St. Mary; St. Peter and Brelade.

A Muster Roll of St. Saviour's Parish in 1617 gives an idea of the armament and composition of a Company. Three Officers, two Sergeants, two Corporals, a Clerk and a Drummer, with two light field pieces with 14 Gunners and Drivers; of the 215 men in the ranks 73 had firearms and 142 halberts and bills; total 238 all ranks, and 2 guns. Each company had its colour carried by an Ensign.

Sir George Carteret, Bailiff and Lt.-Governor, a Royalist, in view of an attack by the Parliamentarians, worked untiringly to improve the efficiency and armament of the companies. The men were mostly armed with match-locks, each Musketeer having to provide himself with 5 lbs. of powder, 60 bullets and a proportion of slow match, besides having to keep his piece in a state of repair and cleanliness.

It was ordered that no matchlock man when carrying arms was to enter a tavern.

When the entire force was paraded it was divided into three groups each of four parishes commanded by a Colonel.

Each Parish had also to raise and equip a small troop of Dragoons for patrolling their own districts by night and day, to be ready to concentrate with the utmost despatch at any point on the coast threatened by an invader. The total number of Dragoons was 150.

Alarm signals were given by ringing church bells, firing guns and lighting beacons.

A description of the Jersey Militia written in 1685 by Jurat Philip Dumaresq gives a complete picture of the force. He says that the Train Bands of the twelve Parishes are formed into three regiments known as the East, North and West Regiments commanded by Colonels, a rank introduced into Jersey some sixty years since. This organization had been perfected by Sir Thomas Morgan, Governor from 1665 to 1679. He divided the Train Bands into 27 companies and allotted 8 to the East, 10 to the North, and 9 to the West Regiment. In addition there was a Troop of Horse of about 60, the total strength of the Island Militia being about 2,500.

The men are generally good shots, better than those of the English Train Bands.

Sir Thomas Morgan did much to improve the discipline of the men and trained them "to march in good order and often took them as far as one day's march would permit, it is a pity he could not have kept them at it for days together, like the English Train Bands are; for our men are not used to be away from their homes at night, as it is possible that an enemy's fleet might cruise round the Island before attempting a landing, and our men should be practised in remaining out, and arrangements made to feed them while out. Their inability to provide themselves with more than one day's food at a time still detracts from their efficiency." Another inconvenience is the variety of firearms for ordinary bullets are not suited to many of the bores, besides firelocks and fowling pieces are apt to get out of order and misfire more frequently than matchlocks.

The twelve Parishes own 24 field pieces which Morgan brigaded under one officer called the controller of the artillery. During the past sixty years some guns have been changed, but some remain which are over one hundred years old. The guns are of two patterns, Falcons and Robinets. The Falcons weigh about 8 cwts, and quite serviceable. The Robinets only weigh 2 or 3 cwts. apiece and throw a $\frac{1}{2}$ lb. shot. They are of little service. Each gun has its own tumbril and horses, smiths and carpenters, but the men who attend them are of the poorest sort and unable to maintain small arms. They number about 300 in all.

In addition to the field guns which are housed in the parish churches, there are some demi-culverins mounted on various parts of the coast. There were seven thus mounted, but four were taken to Elizabeth Castle. They throw a $9\frac{1}{2}$ lb. shot and weigh $3\frac{1}{2}$ cwts.

Seventeen watch houses exist in places which command wide views of the sea, but are now in a state of ruin. Fort St. Aubin is garrisoned by 3 or 4 files of musketeers drawn in turns from the parish companies and commanded by a Sergeant who always lives there.

In 1675, Feb. 2nd, every Militia man was ordered to provide himself with a red casaque at his own expense and to wear it on all parades and duties. The order was fairly well obeyed, as out of St. Peter's company in 1692 only four men out of 92 are without the casaque rouge. No mention is made of hats or leg wear.

From the following Actes des Etats de Jersey for the years 1679 to 1692 all mention the Militia of the Island as being dressed in red cassocks or coats. There were also Troops of mounted Militia dressed in red coats.

Feb. 10th, 1679. Under the Governorship of Sir Thomas Morgan "Sur la proposition faite aux Etats par Monsieur le Gouveneur combien il seroit necessaire pour faire paroestre la Milice de cette isle en bon etat et posture de deffense que tous ceux des divers Regiments qui composent fusent vestus de casaques rouges. Il est expressement enjoint a tous et un chacun de ceux qui sont obligés de fournir et porter armes pour le service du Roy et la defense du pais qu'ils ayent au plustot a se pourvoir de casaques rouges affin que les compagnies en paroessent uniformement couverts aux prochaines montres" (the next inspections).

March 24th, 1688. Sir Thomas Windham, Lt.-Governor. "Monsieur Le Lieut.-Govern^r ayant fait voir aux Etats combien il seroit necessaire pour faire paroestre ceux qui montent les chevaux a la troupe en bon equipage quils fusent vestus de casaques rouges, aussi bien que le reste de la Milice du Pais. Il est expressement enjoint a tous ceux qui sont obligés de fournir des chevaux a la Troupe quils ayent au plutot a se pourvoir de casaques rouges affin que tous les cavaliers en paroissent uniformement couverts a la prochaine montre."

The next order concerns the distribution of vraic (seaweed) saying that every man who fournishes a musket, sword and bandolier or cartouch box and who appears at inspections and guards in his red casaque and armed with his firelock, is to have two portions in distribution of vraic.

Feb. 1st, 1692. "Que chaque home fournisant mousquet lespée et bandolière ou cartouche propre pour le service de leurs Ma^{tes} et paroestra aux montres et à la Garde avec une cassaque rouge portant son dit mousquet luy meme, aura deux lots dans le partage des vrecqs."

1698. "Cavallerie" Militia mentioned.

BIBLIOGRAPHY

History of the British Army. SIR SIBBALD SCOTT.
Hall's Chronicles of Henry VIII.
Stow's Chronicles, 1565.
Military Antiquities. GROSE. 1812.
Armour. ASHDOWN.
Armour. MEYRICK AND SKELTON.
The Souldiers Exercise, The Souldiers Accidence and The Souldiers Grammer. GERVASE MARK-
    HAM, 1643.
Pallas Armata. H. TURNER. 1653.
Principals of The Art Military. CAPTAIN HEXHAM. 1642.
Tangier, 1661–1684. E. G. M. ROUTH.
Graham of Claverhouse. G. M. BARRINGTON.
Rupert Prince Palatine. EVA SCOTT.
History of the British Standing Army, 1660–1700. COLONEL CLIFFORD WALTON, C.B.
History of the Queen's Royal Regiment. LT.-COLONEL J. DAVIS.
The Compleat Gentleman Soldier. 1700.
Marlborough and the Rise of the British Army. C. T. ATKINSON, M.A.
The Wars of Marlborough. FRANK TAYLOR.
A Short Life of Marlborough. HENRY JOHN EDWARDS, C.B.
Life of John Duke of Marlborough. THOMAS LEDIARD. 1736.
Life of the Duke of Marlborough. W. COXE. 1845.
Memoires of the Most Remarkable Transactions, 1683–1718. CAPTAIN ROBERT PARKER.
Camp Discipline, 1666–1736. GENERAL KANE. Published 1743.
A Journal of the Campaign in Flanders, 1708. JOHN MARSHALL DEANE, 1st Foot Guards.
Marlborough, His Life and Times. RT. HON. WINSTON S. CHURCHILL.
Article on "Elixem" in *The Cavalry Journal.* MAJOR FITZ M. STACKE, M.C.
The Story of the Horse. MAJOR A. J. LAMB, D.S.O.
Britain's Sea Soldiers. COLONEL C. FIELD.
Historical Records of the Royal Marine Forces. MAJOR L. EDYE.
History of the Buffs. CAPTAIN H. R. KNIGHT.
The Rise of Military Music. H. G. FARMER.
History of the Coldstream Guards. COLONEL MACKINNON. 1833.
History of the Scots Guards. MAJOR GENERAL SIR FREDERICK MAURICE, K.C.M.G., C.B.
MS History of the English Army. COLONEL JACKSON; in the Royal United Service Institution.
The Journal of the Army Historical Research Society.
History of the 16th Foot. MAJOR SIR FREDERICK MAURICE, K.C.M.G., C.B.
Cavalry. LT.-COLONEL F. N. MAUDE.
    For most of the information regarding pay, administration and the Clothing Board,
I am greatly indebted to SIR JOHN FORTESCUE'S *History of the British Army* and GENERAL
FORBES'S *History of the Ordnance Services.*

BIBLIOGRAPHY

SCOTTISH REGIMENTS

Old Scottish Regimental Colours. ANDREW ROSS.
The Scots Army. C. DALTON.
The Lowland Scots Regiments. SIR HERBERT MAXWELL, BART.
The Military History of Perthshire, 1660–1902. THE MARCHIONESS OF TULLIBARDINE (now
  THE DUCHESS OF ATHOLL, D. B. E.)
The Highland Bag-Pipe. W. L. MANSON.
The Scots Brigade in Holland. JAMES FERGUSON.
The Great Clan Tartan Myth. LT.-COLONEL M. M. HALDANE. Published in *The Scots
  Magazine.*

STANDARDS AND COLOURS

Military Discipline. CAPTAIN THOMAS VENN. 1672.
The Compleat Body of the Art Military. LT.-COLONEL ELTON. 1659.
L'art Militaire François. 1697.
Standards and Colours. S. M. MILNE.

ARTILLERY AND ENGINEERS

Military Discipline, or the Young Artilleryman. 1643.
The Compleat Gunner. CAPTAIN THOMAS VENN. 1672.
Memoires D'artillerie. M. SURIREY DE ST. REMY. 1697.
History of the Royal Regiment of Artillery. COLONEL FRANCIS DUNCAN.
Notes on the Early History of the Royal Regiment of Artillery. G. COLONEL CLEAVELAND.
List of Officers of the Royal Regiment of Artillery. LIEUTENANT KANE.
History of the Dress of the Royal Regiment of Artillery. CAPTAIN MACDONALD.
History of the Corps of Royal Engineers. MAJOR-GENERAL WHITWORTH PARKER.
A Short History of the Royal Regiment of Artillery. J. LOUGHLIN.

MILITIA, TRAIN BANDS, THE HONOURABLE ARTILLERY COMPANY

The Constitutional Force. COLONEL G. JACKSON HAY, C.B., C.M.G.
History of the Honourable Artillery Company. LT.-COLONEL G. A. RAIKES.
History of the Honourable Artillery Company. MAJOR G. GOOLD WALKER, D.S.O., M.C.
Compendium of Military Discipline as it is Practised by the Honourable Artillery Company. JOHN
  BLACKWELL. 1726.
Various Histories of Militia Regiments.

For the Jersey Militia I am grateful for Notes and Material supplied by N. V. L. RYBOT.

INDEX

INDEX

INDEX

INDEX

INDEX